How To
Make any Divorce
Better!

SECOND EDITION

Specific steps

to make things

smoother,

faster,

less painful

and save you

a LOT of money

ED SHERMAN

Best-selling author of *How to Do Your Own Divorce*

Nolo Press
OCCIDENTAL
Carlsbad, CA

Nolo Press Occidental
2604 El Camino Real, Suite 353B
Carlsbad, CA 92008-1297
(831) 466-9922

ISBN: 978-0-944508-96-1
Library of Congress Control Number: 2014951532

ABOUT THE AUTHOR—
Until 2007, Ed Sherman has been a family law attorney since 1967. He founded Nolo Press in 1971 with *How to Do Your Own Divorce in California* and forever changed the way legal services are delivered through his many books on divorce, creation of the independent paralegal movement, and co-founding of Divorce Helpline. He has made it his life's work to help people keep their family problems out of the legal grinder—our adversarial court system.

*I have done my best to ensure the accuracy and usefulness of information in this book, but it is not intended to be a substitute for personal advice from a good family law attorney. Rather, it is about how to avoid using an attorney or using one in a limited capacity and choosing the right one. It is about things you can do yourself that are better than anything an attorney can do for you. No warranty is made, express or implied, and neither **Nolo Press Occidental** nor I assume any liability in connection with any use or result from use of the information contained in this book.—Ed Sherman*

COVER AND INTERIOR DESIGN: DOTTI ALBERTINE
COVER AND INTERIOR PHOTOS: JUPITER IMAGES & ISTOCKPHOTO

Printed in the United States of America.

❝ No matter what your situation, if you follow my advice things will soon get better. ❞

I want you to know why I am so confident that this book will help you. This has been my life's work, helping people avoid unnecessary upset and expense when going through a divorce. So these pages are me speaking to you as directly and sincerely as one can in a book.

My advice is based on over 40 years of experience with over 45,000 cases and millions helped through my books, and I also include concepts from dozens of professional studies. The advice in this book is tried and tested. It has helped thousands of others and it will help you.

"In a time of turbulence and change
. . . knowledge is power."

—John F. Kennedy (1962)
paraphrasing Francis Bacon (1597)

National Awards

- **The Benjamin Franklin Award for Excellence**
  Make Any Divorce Better is an updated and rewritten version of *Practical Divorce Solutions*, which in 1988 was granted the Benjamin Franklin Award by the Independent Bookseller's Association.

- **The USA National Best Books 2008 Award**
  USA Book News named *Make Any Divorce Better* the Winner in Parenting and Family: Divorce.

- **The Library Journal—Best "How-To" 2008**
  LJ first awarded *Make Any Divorce Better* their highly coveted red-star for highly recommended books, then named it one of the Best How-To Books of 2008.

- **ForeWord Magazine 2008 Book of the Year Finalist**

- **Independent Publisher Book Awards 2009**
  Silver Medal awarded to *Make Any Divorce Better*

CONTENTS

Foreword
by Warren Farrell, Ph.D.

*"I have never read a book that has a clearer understanding
of why asking the legal system to resolve divorce is
like asking a boxing coach to be our marriage counselor."*

THE LAW IS BINARY: WIN OR LOSE. With men and women, when either sex wins, both sexes lose.

When a crime is committed, the law can dole out consequences that serve to warn others to not cross the line. For crimes, legal consequences can create security for all. But a marriage that has ended in divorce is no crime. And divorce is its own consequence.

The divorce is a moment in our life's journey in which the appearance of marital security becomes the reality of insecurity in search of renewed security. When a law court makes either sex win, few families experience renewed security.

Divorce is the dream of being swept away being swept away. Lawyers and divorce courts are not in the business of dream recovery. Or repairing the wounds of anger. Or of helping couples understand the vulnerability lying beneath anger: that anger is vulnerability's mask.

Why? A binary system cannot do justice to nuance. A marriage is a person with a complex family history of hopes and fears aspiring to create a union with another person with a complex family history of hopes and fears. From each person's history and genes, emanate securities and insecurities that result in feelings that are either expressed or repressed, then either heard, distorted or ignored, resulting in frustrations, body language and tones of voice which no court can track.

When we ask a court to track it all, we forfeit our privacy, empty our bank account, increase our pain, reinforce our mistrust, and therefore place our future in greater jeopardy. If we have children, we have spread our cancer to them.

I have never read a book that has a clearer understanding of why asking the legal system to resolve divorce is like asking a boxing coach to be our marriage counselor. To paraphrase Ed Sherman, the legal system is adversarial, and therefore lawyers argue to fight and win. As Sherman puts it, "More fighting and arguing is probably not what you need."

There
handle pai
marriage t
when supp
more conv
we are to c
are to beco
here is why
long run…
The jol
successful i
and theref
looking for
pass on to
heal. That's
worse the j
When
vulture ma
recycling sy
to heal wil
legal systen
offering a r
have no ho
gift when v

DR. WARREN F
Women Can't
His Father and
after divorce. **I**
has appeared f
subject of two s
100 thought le
in *Business We*
Report. Learn n

Peggy Williams, Anne Lober, and **Charma Pipersky,** attorneys and mediators, former partners in Divorce Helpline, for their valuable critique, fresh ideas and priceless friendship.

Hamid Naraghi, attorney, mediator, Private Judge, President of Divorce Helpline, friend and one of the finest human beings I know, for carrying on the good work and helping so many thousands of California couples find a safe and sane way through a treacherous passage.

And special thanks go to **Kenneth Kressel,** author of *The Process of Divorce: How Professionals and Couples Negotiate Divorce.* This readable academic study gathered together everything known about divorce settlements in the literature of social science and provided an invaluable supplement to my own professional experience.

TRIAGE
– What to do first

General rule 1. Unless there's an emergency, do not talk to an attorney (or continue, if you've started) until you've read clear to the end of chapter 6 and learned:

- the huge difference between *retaining* an attorney or just using one
- what an attorney can and cannot do for you
- exactly what you want from the attorney
- how to organize your facts and questions you want answered
- why in most cases you should minimize the attorney's role
- how mediation solves problems so much better than going to court
- how to pick the right kind of help for your case (if any is needed)

General rule 2. Try to avoid talking to your spouse about divorce until you've read through chapter 6.

General rule 3. Any time you feel you want to talk to someone rather than continue with this book, read chapter 7, *I want someone to help me—Who can I call?*

In medicine, *triage* means to prioritize patients by the severity of their condition. This is what we are doing in this section—deciding what your situation is and how to get from wherever you are to where you belong in this book. Find yourself in the sections below. Skip those that are not about you.

A. Emergencies

1. **Fear for the safety of yourself or your child.** If your spouse is an habitual controller/abuser—that is, has abused several times in the past—and you fear it will happen again, read chapter 1D, *Domestic Abuse and Violence.* You need advice from a DV counselor and you need to find a safe place to go.

2. **Divorce papers served on you.** This may or may not be a real emergency. If you've been served with papers and you want to have some say in the outcome, you need to file a response before the deadline stated on your papers. If it has passed, call the court clerk and ask if you are still able to file a response even though the deadline has passed. If so, quickly file a response. If not, you'll need an attorney to help you make a motion to allow you to enter the case late. In either situation, read chapter 7 about how to find the right kind of help.

   If a hearing has been scheduled in the near future to determine support or child custody issues, you need to get an attorney right away to either represent you at the hearing or seek a continuance so you can prepare. Read chapter 7 about what kind of attorney you want. If you don't have time to get an attorney, show up in court at the time and place indicated on your papers and ask the judge for a continuance so you can get an attorney.

   Even if you are in litigation, you should still read this book and look for ways to move the action out of court and into mediation. Mediation and its advantages are in discussed in chapter 5E.

3. **Fear of sneak attack.** If you think your spouse might launch a sneak attack in court—seeking orders for custody and support before you do—or just take the kids and the money and run, or both, read chapter 5 and decide if you are going to be defensive or take the offense first.

4. **Desperately broke.** Most people worry about how bills will get paid when the same income has to support two households, but if your money situation is truly desperate and frightening—*or if your spouse feels this way*—read chapter 6, step 4, then consider your options.

B. Already in litigation

If you are already in a legal struggle with attorneys on both sides, read chapter 2, *The divorce road map*; chapter 5, *Strategies;* chapter 9, *How to win a legal battle*; and chapter 7, *I want someone to help me—Who can I call?* Then resume back here and read through the book with an eye to finding a way out of litigation and into either mediation or collaborative divorce.

C. Everyone else

Whatever is on your mind, either the answer lies just ahead or advice about how to get the answers or the help you most need. Go on to the summary, then chapter 1, *Which Divorce Profile Fits You?*, and continue from there. Let the book be your guide.

SUMMARY
– The book in a nutshell

1. To get a divorce, you need a judgment dissolving your marriage and, if you have marital property, debts or children, you will need orders regarding:

   a. Division of marital assets and debts
   b. Spousal support, if any
   c. If there are children, parenting arrangements and child support
   d. If conflict is very high, restraining orders to help keep the peace

   That's all. This is the sum and total of what the legal divorce is about.

2. If you're having trouble, it is almost certainly not legal. Almost all divorce problems are due to upset, relationship issues, or poor communication.

3. While the legal system can be useful in emergencies or if your spouse is an habitual abuser/controller, the law has **no tools** to help solve relationship problems—none, not any—so attorneys you hire to take your case also lack tools to solve relationship problems. Apart from getting emergency orders for desperate situations, the law and attorneys who represent you *in the legal system* are useless to a divorcing couple. This is why many attorneys are choosing to work *outside* the legal system by becoming mediators or by representing people in a new format called "collaborative law" (see chapters 5E and 7).

4. If you retain an attorney to represent you, to take your case, you will invariably end up in the legal system and things will get worse instead of better. This is because our

legal system is based on the *adversarial* model, where parties are regarded as enemies in a battle who are fighting to win the best judgment. Attorneys fight and argue trying to win. More fighting and arguing is probably not what you need. If you want to be represented anyway, get an attorney who practices collaborative law (chapter 7).

5. If you care about privacy, court records are public, so every detail will be open to anyone who cares to look. If handled out of court, most details of your divorce can be kept private.

6. The secret to a successful divorce is to minimize your use of the legal system and of the kind of attorneys who work in it.

    a. Unless you have an emergency: (i) don't go to an attorney before you are informed and prepared (by reading through to chapter 6, step 7) and (ii) don't retain an attorney to handle your divorce.

    b. If you need legal information or assistance, learn how to use an attorney safely and effectively in a limited and defined way.

    c. Learn how to choose the right kind of attorney for what you need.

    d. Learn how and when other professionals can be far more useful.

7. When it comes to solving divorce problems, the things you can do yourself are more effective than anything an attorney can do for you, which is what much of this book is about—reducing conflict, solving problems, reducing your exposure to lawyers and court.

8. A few cases, not so many as you might think, are not suitable for a peaceful approach because one or both of the parties is likely to do something underhanded or even violent. So, if you are going to fight, you might as well learn how to fight effectively. That's in here, too.

9. No matter what your situation, this book will show you everything you need to know to get on the best path to a smoother divorce.

1

WHICH DIVORCE PROFILE FITS YOU?

THIS CHAPTER WILL GUIDE YOU to the information and advice in this book that you need. Read through the profiles below and find out which one fits you best, then follow the directions found there. If you feel uncertain and can't tell where you fit, just read straight through this book and soon you will know.

If you don't know what you are doing, it is very easy to make any divorce worse.

FIVE DIVORCE PROFILES—which one fits you?
Early • Easy • Difficult • Domestic Abuse • Legal Battle

> If you don't know what you are doing, it is very easy to make any divorce worse. An easy case can become difficult and a difficult case can turn into a war. But if you follow my advice, any divorce can be made better, even if you're at war. The steps you take depend on what stage you are in, what kind of divorce you have.

A. Early or uncertain

You broke up recently or haven't broken up yet. It might be too soon to tell what kind of divorce you are headed for, but reading this book will make things clear. Keep in mind that "as the twig is bent, so grows the tree." The way you do things now will have a powerful influence on how things unfold in the future—for better or worse.

These early days are a golden opportunity to shape your future, a chance to lay the groundwork for a smooth trip ahead. For most people, your goal is to end up with an Easy Divorce (below) where there is no legal opposition.

A small percentage of cases are not suitable for a peaceful approach. If you fear your spouse might strike first with a sudden legal action, or do something underhanded, like grab the kids and the money and run, then you can't leave yourself vulnerable while you are working toward a peaceful solution. This is a crucial decision point—will you try to make your divorce go smoothly or strike first and start a war? Will you be on offense or defense, or something in between? The way you answer this question can affect you for the rest of your life. It's the choice between war or peace. If this is an open question for you, read chapter 5 on strategy right after you finish this chapter.

You'll be repaid a thousand times for what you accomplish at this stage.

Your decision is entirely based on your personal assessment of your spouse's likely behavior, so if your own state of mind is in turmoil, you should consider getting independent neutral advice from a family law mediator who also does some litigation. See chapter 7. If you feel safe in keeping your divorce out of court while you work on smoothing it out, and if you understand what a terrible disaster it would be for your case to end up in court, then you won't mind taking the time to read this book and put in the effort. You'll be repaid a thousand times for what you accomplish at this stage.

Assuming that you decide as most people will to work toward an out-of-court divorce, here's what to do next.

Do not talk to your spouse about divorce or go to an attorney yet. If you go to an attorney before you are informed and prepared, chances are high that you'll end up in a legal battle. If you need convincing, chapter 2C explains why this is so.

Next:

- Read chapter 3A, *The elements of a good divorce*, for a model of what you are trying to accomplish, then come back here and continue through.

- Read through chapter 6, *Ten steps to a better divorce*, for specific things you can do to plan, prepare and achieve your goal.

If you want to work toward a smooth divorce, read this book to:

- **Create stability and safety** for at least a few months, then help your spouse do the same. You both need time to calm down, read this book, do your homework, think things over and prepare yourself.

A person who is better prepared will almost always do better than one who is not.

- **Learn specific things** you can do to reduce upset and fears about money and parenting.

- **Organize your facts and prepare.** A person who is better prepared will almost always do better than one who is not.

- **Learn how to talk to your spouse** and **ten tips for how to negotiate.**

- **Learn how to get help** if you need it and what kind of help is best for you.

B. The Easy Divorce

In the easy divorce, there will be no legal opposition when you go to court to get your divorce. If you do not have property or want spousal support and have no children, you must tell that to the court. Otherwise you must make decisions and tell the court what you plan to do about:

- the division of marital property and debts
- spousal support, if any, and
- if you have children: custody, visitation and child support.

The reason there will be no opposition in court could be because your spouse is gone, doesn't care or can't be bothered, or because working out the terms of your divorce goes smoothly.

Settlement agreements

An agreement reminds you later what you agreed to and makes it easy for you to get your divorce judgment.

If your spouse is in the picture and if you have marital property or debts to divide, or spousal support is needed, or if you have children to support and parent, it is *much* better to get these things settled in a formal written agreement. Learn how to do this in chapter 6, step 10. An agreement reminds you later what you agreed to and makes it easy for you to get your divorce judgment. If your spouse is long gone or won't participate, you'll have to go on without an agreement.

Three kinds of easy divorce

1. **Absent or uninvolved spouse.** You can get any orders you want because your spouse is gone, doesn't care or can't be bothered. There will be no settlement agreement. To get your divorce, you only need to do some paperwork and go through some red tape at the courthouse. This is something you can do yourself or with inexpensive assistance. Read chapter 8, *How to do your own divorce.*

2. **Easy agreement.** You can work out terms of your divorce on your own or with the help of a mediator (chapter 7) to help you settle things you don't agree on.

3. **Agreement with some effort.** You're having a hard time agreeing to terms, but you can both agree to use a mediator or collaborative lawyers (see chapters 5E and 7) to help you settle the terms of your divorce. You're now on the border between the Easy and the Difficult Divorce, so read that section too, then chapter 4 and chapter 6 to find out things you can do to reduce conflict and make negotiation or mediation work for you, and chapter 7 to find out who can help.

Agreement worksheets. I put agreement and parenting plan worksheets on the CD as a guide and checklist of things you should consider when making your own agreement. Chapter 6, step 10 is about how to put your agreement in writing. Once you have a written agreement, you only need to do some paperwork and go through some red tape to get your judgment. This is something you can do yourself or with inexpensive assistance. Read chapter 8, *How to do your own divorce.* Find out why online forms services are not your best choice.

Don't start your divorce paperwork until your spouse knows it is starting and accepts it.

Keeping an easy divorce easy

Starting the paperwork. Don't start your divorce paperwork until your spouse knows it is starting and accepts it. Don't let papers be served on your spouse in a place where receiving them might be embarrassing or without telling him/her that the papers are coming and you have discussed what steps to expect next. If you are planning to negotiate a written agreement and don't yet have one, give your spouse a signed letter from you, or your attorney if you have one, stating, "I promise you that I will not take any step to advance this case until either we have reached a written agreement or I give you 30 days' written notice that I intend to proceed."

If you and your spouse are in regular contact, flare-ups are a real possibility that you should prepare for. A little reading here might save you a great deal of trouble later if it helps you avoid stirring things up or know how to calm things if they do. Read on through chapter 6, *Ten steps to a better divorce.*

It may be easy, but is it good? Read chapter 3A, *The elements of a good divorce.*

C. The Difficult Divorce

The reason divorces are difficult is almost always about personal relations between you and your spouse, not about the law.

This profile fits most couples and covers a range from almost easy to raging arguments. Your spouse is in the picture and cares how things work out. These cases can be easily stirred up into higher conflict, but if handled correctly at least 85% can be calmed down and settled without legal battle. This book shows you how to do this. The important thing is for you to have the desire to settle your case without a big fight and form that intention. What you expect to happen generally does.

"Difficult" covers everything from a simple inability to agree, to incessant arguing, to terrible emotional outbursts with insults and verbal attacks.

Passive Resistance. A separate kind of difficulty is when a spouse does not argue or fight so much as never engages, never decides, delays and obstructs. If this fits you, be patient and try the advice in this book, but be sure to read about passive resistance in the side article at chapter 6, step 8.

High conflict. At the high end of the difficult range we edge near domestic abuse and violence. Over that line, you are dealing with an habitual abuser/controller, a repeat offender, who is so unlike normal people that advice given here will not be a reliable solution. If you fear for the safety of yourself or your children, read the Domestic Abuse and Violence profile on page 8.

It's personal, not legal. The reason divorces are difficult is almost always about personal relations between you and your spouse, not about the law. The law has no tools whatever—none, not any—to help settle problems based on your personal relationship. There are a lot of things you can do for yourself to make things better, things that are superior to anything a lawyer can do for you. The steps found in chapters 4 and 6 have helped thousands of couples, so they can help you, too.

War or peace? Almost every couple can benefit from working on a peaceful settlement of divorce terms, but there are a few cases (not as many as you might think) where starting off on a peaceful track is not safe because your spouse is the kind of person who is likely to do something bad, like become violent or take the money or the kids and run, so you need to start off with some protection before going to work on trying to move your case toward negotiation or mediation. These situations are discussed in chapter 5B.

There are a lot of things you can do for yourself to make things better, things that are superior to anything a lawyer can do for you.

Strategies for the difficult divorce are discussed at length in chapter 5, but first read chapter 2 to get an overview of the legal system; how it works, how it doesn't, and how to beat it. Don't skip chapter 3, on how to deal with the emotional aspects of divorce and how to reduce conflict and stress. Read chapter 4 if you're interested in laws about property, support and parenting, then do chapter 5, *Strategies for the difficult divorce*.

Do not talk to an attorney or to your spouse about divorce. Unless you have an emergency like those described in chapter 5B, do not talk to your spouse about divorce or take your case to an attorney before you have read this book through chapter 6, *Ten steps to a better divorce*.

D. Domestic Abuse and Violence (DV)

DV covers a range of controlling behavior including physical attacks, threats, intimidation, verbal attacks on a personal level (put-downs, insults, undermining your self-confidence) and other efforts to control you. It can sometimes be difficult to distinguish between high levels of divorce conflict and some forms of domestic abuse and violence.

You need to be sure you aren't creating a legal battle out of your own anger or a desire for revenge, as that would be self-destructive in the extreme.

This profile is about cases where your spouse has been an **habitual** controller/abuser, one who has committed the bad acts repeatedly, not just in the heat of breaking up. Our advice for Difficult Divorces will not be reliable because there's no talking to these people—they don't respond to reason because their need to control or abuse is so strong. When dealing with a controller/abuser, your only choice is to go to a shelter and look for advice and support from counselors who specialize in DV.

Safety first. If you fear for the safety of yourself or a child, go somewhere safe. Visit a friend or relative, someplace where you can't be found. If you need help with planning your escape, ask local police to refer you to domestic abuse support groups near you. Once you are safe, what you need most now is personal advice and counseling from someone who specializes in domestic abuse situations. Restraining orders are effective against the majority of offenders, though not all. Get help.

You are the one who knows best the kind of person your spouse is. If in doubt, play it safe. Once you are safe, read the profile below and chapters 3 and 9.

E. Legal Battle

You need to be sure you aren't creating a legal battle out of your own anger or a desire for revenge, as that would be self-destructive in the extreme. But there are cases where you simply can't avoid a legal battle or where you decide it's best not to (chapter 5B). If you think your spouse might take off with the kids or the money while you are trying to work things out, or if your spouse is a controller/abuser, you might benefit from legal assistance. If your spouse gets an attorney who resists taking the case into mediation or who you can't negotiate with constructively or whose demands are intolerably beyond reason, then you pretty much have to do what you have to do: get an attorney of your own and fight back. How to choose the right kind of attorney is discussed in chapter 7. Read this book to find out all the things you can do to move your case toward negotiation or mediation and keep trying for that result.

If you have to fight, you might as well learn how to do it effectively, so welcome to the Battle Group. Notice that the title says "legal" battle—you do not need to battle on a personal or emotional level. In fact, it is better if you do not. But you do need to read chapter 9, *How to win a legal battle,* to learn:

If you have to fight, you might as well learn how to do it effectively.

- How to deal with extreme conflict
- Damage control
- Protecting your children
- Winning strategies—hardball or softball?
- How to fight effectively at less expense
- How to choose and use your attorney
- How to fire your attorney (if you want to)

F. Steps to take in every case

Practical steps. For a list of things everyone should do at the earliest opportunity, read chapter 6, step 3, *Early practical steps.* In addition to preparation and planning, at some early stage you need to close joint accounts, cancel joint credit cards, establish your own credit, plan how you will get by for the next few months, and so on. If you are in touch with your spouse (and aren't planning a surprise attack) let him/her know what you are doing in time to make other arrangements for accounts, credit cards, and so on.

Being organized and prepared has many advantages in even the simplest case.

Organize your facts. Use the worksheets on the CD that comes with this book to organize the personal and financial facts of your case. Being organized and prepared has many advantages in even the simplest case. The worksheets not only help you make sure you've thought of everything, they organize information and documents you will need when you go to court to get your divorce judgment. Being informed and prepared will help you every step of the way and it needs to be done, so start as soon as you can. Read chapter 6, step 6, *Get Organized*, and the Appendix, *How to get the information you need.*

2

THE DIVORCE ROAD MAP
– Overview of the Legal Divorce

A. Crossing the great divide

TO BEAT THE LEGAL SYSTEM, you first have to see it, see how it works, get an overview.

Think of your divorce as having to go on a difficult journey across unknown, rugged territory—something like the early settlers faced when they had to get across the real Great Divide, the terrifying Rocky Mountains. Behind you is a life you can no longer live. Before you is a future with more hope and possibilities, but first you have to get across an unknown terrain full of traps, dangers and pitfalls. You stand there with your life's accumulations, fighting fear, trying to find the means and the courage to go into the unknown, when suddenly someone shows up with a map and book full of information and advice about your journey. That's us.

Divorce might not be easy, but you certainly don't have to go blindly or alone. Others have already marked the best paths and if you take a popular route there will be traveler's services and reliable guides. What you need to do now is study the maps and the travel information before you start. You don't want to just wander off into your divorce, you want to go informed and prepared.

You don't want to just wander off into your divorce, you want to go informed and prepared.

B. The divorce road map

The real divorce is your life, the context in which the narrow concerns of the legal divorce are played out. It is about ending one life and beginning another. It's about your relationships with your Ex, family, friends, children and yourself. It's what you go through in practical, emotional and spiritual terms. The real divorce is about breaking old patterns, finding a new center for your life and doing your best with the hand you've been dealt. These matters are not assisted or addressed in any way by the legal divorce. Chapter 3 discusses your real divorce and how to get through it.

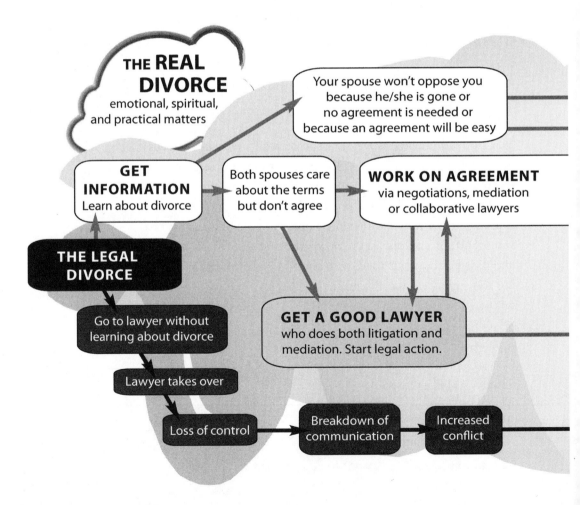

The legal divorce is only about settling the division of marital property, support and parenting. In high conflict cases, it's also about keeping the peace. That's all, nothing more. If you could settle these matters out of court, there would be nothing left but some paperwork and red tape to get your judgment, yet this is the arena in which people experience so much frustration and expense. Why is that?

Problems in a divorce are almost never legal, almost always about personalities and emotions, for which there are absolutely **no** solutions in court or in a lawyer's office—zip, zero, nothing. In fact,

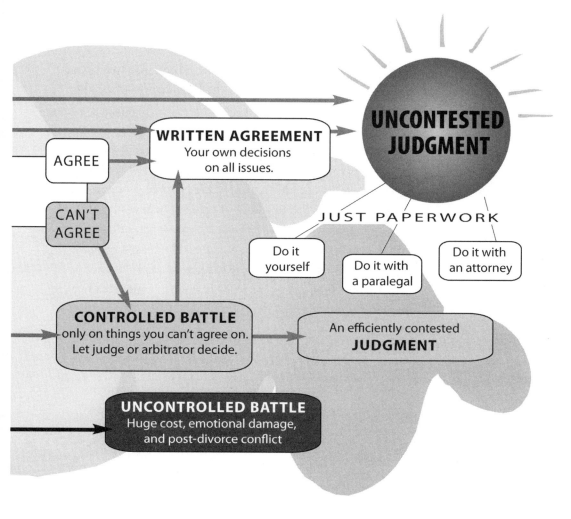

getting involved with lawyers and courts almost always makes things worse instead of better. The purpose of this book is to guide you to solutions that reduce your exposure to the legal grinder or, if you can't avoid a legal battle, how to conduct it effectively.

The worst path. Unless you have an immediate emergency, going to a lawyer without first becoming informed and prepared is the worst thing you can possibly do! The tools available to a lawyer are almost certainly going to make your case worse rather than better. The likelihood for unnecessary pain and expense is very high. If you have already started on this path, it may not be too late to change course and try to get on one of the better routes—but sooner is better. As you go further along it becomes harder to get off.

Two best paths—knowing where you are going. The two better routes both start when you learn how the legal divorce works then develop your best options.

Problems in a divorce are almost never legal, almost always about personalities and emotions, for which there are absolutely no solutions in court or in a lawyer's office—zip, zero, nada, niente, nothing.

• **Unopposed cases.** Cases where there is no legal opposition in court are relatively easy, so this is your best path if you can get on it. This fits the Easy Divorce profile in chapter 1. If you have this kind of case, you can easily do your own divorce (chapter 8) with a book or kit, or do it with the inexpensive assistance of a divorce typing service, or get a family law attorney-mediator to draft an agreement for you, then get the paperwork done in court. Read chapter 7 about who can help.

• **Cases with disagreement.** This is the Difficult Divorce profile in chapter 1 and describes most cases. Your goal is to get through it as smoothly as possible, using the steps in this book through chapter 6 to move your case toward a negotiated or mediated settlement. True, a small percentage of cases are not amenable to a peaceful approach and require legal action before moving toward settlement, but before you decide to take a hard approach or get a lawyer to handle your case, read chapter 5, *Strategies for the difficult divorce,* and then on through chapter 6. Most people stumble into a legal battle without intending to, usually by going straight to a lawyer and putting the case in the lawyer's hands. Don't do that. Unless you have an emergency, don't go to an attorney without first becoming informed and prepared by reading through this book. If you do feel forced (or were forced) to take action to protect yourself, then read this book as soon as you can and learn how to take more control over how your case is conducted. Try to move your case toward mediation and/or arbitration.

A third path—controlled battle. This is what happens if you decide not to work toward an agreement because you feel the need to first protect yourself, or if you have tried and can't settle terms. A controlled battle is a legal contest conducted with lawyers, but you know what is going on, the issues of disagreement are well defined and you are the one calling the shots. The worst outcome on this path is still better and cheaper than what you are likely to get from going uninformed and unprepared to an attorney and letting him/her take over your case and your life.

C. How the law works against you

If there were no legal system, no lawyers and no courts, divorce would still be difficult and it would still take time to go through it. But we *do* have a legal system—a mostly harmful one when it comes to family matters. Here you are, you and your spouse, going through difficult personal life changes when the State comes along and says, "Excuse me! You can't do this without us. Your divorce has to be conducted under our rules, and you can't even hope to understand our rules. By the way, our system has no tools for helping you solve personal problems or negotiate with your spouse. In fact, it is based on conflict and is specially designed to cause trouble and greatly increase your expense. Please pay your filing fees on the way in."

Most people stumble into a legal battle without intending to, usuallly by going straight to a lawyer and putting the case in the lawyer's hands. Don't do that.

We have an "adversarial" system. It began in the Middle Ages with "trial by combat," where men with a disagreement would fight and he who survived was "right." Today, physical contact is no longer a recognized legal technique, but things are still set up as a fight. The parties are regarded as adversaries, enemies in combat. In a divorce, the spouses and their attorneys argue against one another and try to "win" the case, to "beat" the opposition. Rules of professional conduct require your attorney to be "adversarial," that is, aggressive and combative. This system and the way lawyers work in it is a major cause of trouble and the high cost of divorce. You want to have as little as possible to do with it.

Lawyers are not always villains. Conflict is already lively in most divorces and lawyers are sometimes more moderate than their clients. But even for lawyers who mean well, the tools they use and the system they work in will usually increase conflict, because that's the nature of the system they work in.

This system and the way lawyers work in it is a major cause of trouble and the high cost of divorce.

Professional rules of practice forbid your lawyer from communicating directly with your spouse. It is expected that your spouse will be represented by an attorney and your lawyer can only communicate through your spouse's lawyer. Your attorney can't "talk sense" to your spouse, or explain how you see things. This means your attorney will always have a one-sided view of your case and can never achieve an understanding any greater than your own. This means that instead of two people who can't talk to each other you have four people who can't talk to each other.

How it works. Look at the diagram on the next page and you'll see that every divorce starts with a petition and ends with a judgment and there are only three possible paths for getting from one to the other.

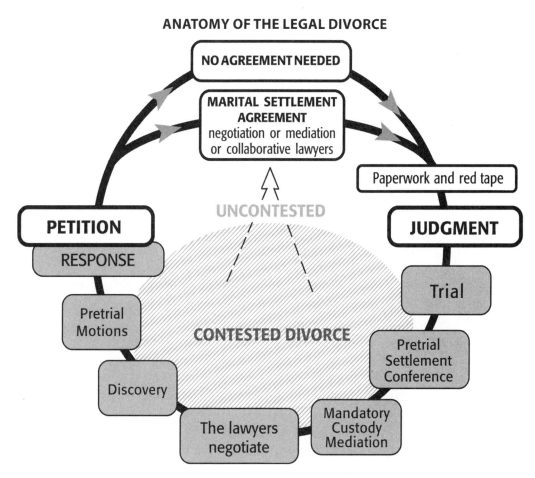

ANATOMY OF THE LEGAL DIVORCE

Pretrial motions: Formal motions and hearings to get temporary orders on such things as support, custody, visitation, possession of family home, keep-away, non-molest, freeze assets, prevent sale or waste of assets.

Discovery: A variety of legal tools to dig for information about assets or other issues. Depositions (taking of statements under oath), interrogatories (sworn answers in writing to questions), and demands for copies of documents.

Negotiations: Spouse's lawyers seek written agreements on as many facts and issues as possible. Not a formal part of the system.

Mandatory custody mediation: Some states require parenting classes for all parents and mediation if they can't agree on child custody and parenting arrangements. If mediation doesn't work, the judge may require a home study and report by a court-appointed counselor.

Pretrial settlement conference: An informal meeting with lawyers, clients and a judge who will give an opinion on likely rulings and try to pressure (persuade) parties to settle without trial.

Settlement agreement: A written contract to settle all issues. Strongly recommended in any case with significant property, debts or minor children.

Terms may vary from state to state, but divorces are similar in all states. In this book, we use the first set of terms.

· Spouse who starts the divorce	=	Petitioner	or Plaintiff
· Document filed	=	Petition	or Complaint
· The other spouse	=	Respondent	or Defendant
· Document filed (if any)	=	Response	or Answer
· Orders for divorce and terms	=	Judgment	or Decree

If you don't need an agreement or if you can work out an agreement by negotiation or with the help of a mediator, it can be easy and inexpensive to get your judgment.

Contested divorce. The lower half of the round diagram on the previous page shows what an attorney can and will do if you retain him/her to handle your divorce because these are the only tools available to an attorney who works in the legal system. The legal system is so unsuitable that many attorneys have left it in favor of becoming a mediator or engaging in a new form of practice called collaborative law where attorneys on both sides agree in writing not to go to court or threaten to go to court but rather seek settlement through negotiation, mediation and possibly counseling.

Everything becomes easy once you have a written settlement agreement. Even if you are in a legal contest, you can leave it at any time by negotiating or mediating an agreement.

Divorce by agreement. Everything becomes easy once you have a settlement agreement. Even if you are in a legal contest, you can leave it at any time by negotiating or mediating an agreement. Chapters 4 and 6 show you things you can do yourself to work toward an agreement. If you have trouble working out terms on your own, get a mediator. If one or both of you prefer to be represented, you can each get your own collaborative law attorney. None of these approaches involves the terrible emotional and financial cost of fighting in court. See chapter 7 about the different kinds of help that are available and how to choose.

Emergencies. If you have or fear an emergency (see chapter 5B), an attorney can make motions for temporary support, custody and restraining orders to protect people or property, or use discovery to get documents and information. For such purposes legal action might make sense, but many attorneys use legal action routinely, whether your case requires it or not, stirring things up and increasing their fees. If you and your spouse can work out your own temporary arrangements and share all information openly, you'll have no need for incredibly expensive legal tools. You can keep your case out of lawyers' offices and out of court.

If either spouse is represented by an attorney, that attorney will write letters, file legal papers, make motions, and do discovery. These actions will compel the other spouse get an attorney, too, and at that point your case has become contested and the cost and conflict level will go up. Their negotiation techniques tend to be combative so soon you'll have a hotly contested case, lots of cost, and a couple of very upset spouses. Fees in contested cases can run from tens of thousands of dollars each all the way up to everything you own or can borrow.

D. How to beat the legal system

Of course you want to get your judgment—that's your legal divorce—but unless you have an emergency or high conflict or if your spouse is likely to do something underhanded (see chapter 5B), the legal system has little to offer and you don't want to suffer through it. You do not want to get tangled up with lawyers and courts, so instead of going through the legal system, you go around it. You work outside the legal system to make arrangements and reach an agreement with your spouse, just as shown on the diagram on page 17. If necessary, get limited assistance in the form of information and advice from attorneys who do not represent you. Get a professional mediator to help you work out your terms. If you feel better being represented, get attorneys on each side who practice collaborative law. See chapter 7, *I want someone to help me—Who can I call?*

If you and your spouse can work out your own temporary arrangements and share all information openly, you'll have no need for incredibly expensive legal tools.

Doing things yourself, you have far more control and better solutions. Working outside the system is the way you get a low conflict, low impact, high-quality divorce.

Retaining vs. using an attorney. To stay outside the legal system, neither spouse should retain an attorney unless there is an emergency. The key word is retain. This doesn't mean you can't get help from an attorney, just that you should not retain one unless you have no other choice. If you follow the methods in this book, you might not need any help from an attorney at all, but if you do, you'll know how to limit the help you get and who to call.

Retaining an attorney means the attorney takes professional responsibility for, and control of, your case. To retain an attorney, you sign a retainer agreement that creates a relationship where—and attorneys never mention this—if you have more trouble the attorney makes more money! This is not conducive to cost-effective service.

Working outside the legal system is the way you get a low conflict, low impact, high-quality divorce.

You will typically be asked to pay some amount "on retainer" and your attorney has now taken over control of your case. This is what they mean when they say, "I'll take your case." And they do take your case—right into the high-conflict, low-solution legal system. The attorney retainer is the poison apple—don't bite it.

Because you want to minimize your use of a system that works so hard against you, you must not retain an attorney unless you have no choice, but you do need to retain an attorney if you are facing immediate threat of harm. You need an attorney if you:

• Have good reason to believe your spouse poses a danger to you, your children or your property or can be expected to do something underhanded, like clean out your accounts, take the kids and run

- Can't get support from your spouse and have no way to live

- Think your spouse is transferring, selling or hiding assets

In such cases, read chapters 3 and 6 then get an attorney right away. In all other cases, you only want an attorney for information and advice or possibly to perform one limited service, such as drafting your agreement.

If you feel uneasy about not being represented by an attorney, don't worry; in the rest of this book, you are going to learn very effective things you can do for yourself and how to get useful help if you need it. If you still want to be represented, you will learn in chapter 7 of the possibility of both you and your spouse being represented by *collaborative law* attorneys who will represent you without going to court (see chapter 5E).

The attorney retainer is the poison apple—don't bite it.

3

THE REAL DIVORCE IS FREE

BEFORE DIGGING into the *legal* divorce, let's look at your real divorce—how you feel right now. This is about ending one life and starting another, getting a new center of balance and making it work—spiritually, emotionally and practically.

The state of your emotions has great *practical* significance. In order to make sound decisions—indeed, to solve any problems—you need to be aware of your inner condition and, often, that of your spouse. You need to know how to deal with emotional issues and how not to get stuck in psychological traps. Understanding basic things about how the real divorce works will help you in dealing with yourself, your spouse, your legal divorce and your list of practical problems.

Possibly the most real thing in your life right now is the way you feel. Nothing else is as real as your pain, fear, anger, hurt, guilt, tension, nervousness, illness, depression—whatever it is you are feeling. The practical tasks you face are also very real—how to get by financially, how to rearrange the parenting of your children, what to say to family and friends, what to do next, and so on. Your real divorce, then, presents these challenges:

This is about ending one life and starting another, getting a new center of balance and making it work—spiritually, emotionally and practically.

Emotional. This is about breaking (or failing to break) the bonds, patterns, dependencies, and habits that attach you to your ex-spouse—learning to let go and get beyond anger, fear, hurt, guilt, blame, and resentment. Over time, you learn about past mistakes so you don't have to repeat them; you develop a balanced view of yourself, your ex-spouse, and your marriage; you create self-confidence and an openness to new intimate relationships.

Physical. Our minds and bodies are not separate. Emotions—especially strong ones that are ignored, denied or repressed—are frequently expressed physically. During divorce, people tend to experience a lot of tension, nervousness, and insecurity. They get ill frequently and have accidents. This is a time when you must focus on relaxation and take extra good care of your health.

In contrast to the real divorce, the legal divorce is specifically about property, custody, support and, in high-conflict cases, keeping the peace.

Practical. This is about taking care of business, including your legal divorce. It's the nuts and bolts of what to do, where to go, how to get there as you begin to build a new life for yourself. You need to create safety and security for yourself and your children; to make ends meet in a new lifestyle that produces what you need and needs no more than you can produce—in other words, living within your new level of income.

In contrast to the real divorce, the legal divorce is specifically about property, custody, support and, in high-conflict cases, keeping the peace. Whatever you go through to get it, what you end up with is a bit of paper with court orders written on it. So, what does the legal divorce accomplish for your real divorce? Surprisingly little, as you will see—it is just a subcategory of the practical real divorce. But the legal divorce does have important symbolic value. When you file those papers, it makes an important statement to your spouse, to yourself and to the world that a decision has been made, a new identity and a new direction have been chosen. In practical terms, it forces you to deal with some of your important practical issues (property, custody and support). That's about it for the legal divorce.

The real divorce is what your life is about and how you go about it—this is your real work in life. And unless you decide to get counseling or go into therapy, the real divorce doesn't cost a dime. It is, however, very costly in terms of personal effort, but here, too, you can reduce the cost by learning to avoid common traps. Going through major life changes—in other words, recreating your life—is demanding, painful, hard work, but it may be the most important work you ever do.

A. The elements of a good divorce

I'm starting here so you can see what a good outcome looks like and why it should become your goal. Don't worry if you don't get everything right—few do. Just do your best and get as close as you can. Following this section are tools and tips that can help you on your way.

Experience and academic studies have helped identify the basic elements of a successful emotional divorce. "Successful," as used here, means completing the process of emotional separation, reaching a new center of balance as a single person, maintaining the welfare of your children, and establishing healthy attitudes toward yourself, your ex-spouse, and your past marriage.

Absence of conflict is not part of the ideal divorce. A degree of anger and conflict is natural, useful, even constructive. It helps to break the bonds of attachment and old patterns of relationship; it makes you think and reflect; it makes you change. But excessive and destructive conflict requires special treatment. The discussion of conflict and how to deal with it is in chapter 6, step 9.

Going through major life changes—in other words, recreating your life—is demanding, painful, hard work, but it may be the most important work you ever do.

Apart from peace of mind and personal growth, there are very practical advantages to working hard to make your divorce as good and successful as possible. The closer you can get to ideals described below, the more you will reduce stress and conflict. You will have a greater chance for compliance with terms of any agreements, save thousands in legal costs and, if you have children, you will greatly improve co-parenting and cooperation. In short, everything works better.

The elements of a good divorce

Apart from peace of mind and personal growth, there are very practical advantages to working hard to make your divorce as good and successful as possible.

Mutuality. Lack of sharing in the decision to divorce is the primary cause of conflict in the divorce and post-divorce periods. In an ideal divorce, the decision is arrived at together. This doesn't mean one spouse won't be sadder or more distressed than the other, but that both come to accept divorce as the best thing under the circumstances. The most stable settlements occur when both spouses take an active role in negotiating a settlement, not simply leaving it to a lawyer. A good divorce is an actively mutual enterprise.

Attitude. Each spouse should end up with a balanced view of the other and of the marriage experience. There should be a sense of emotional and spiritual closure. You should be free of any lingering feeling of blame, guilt or failure. You want to create increased self-understanding, the ability to form healthy new intimate relationships, and a sense of self-confidence.

Children. In an ideal divorce, injury to children is minimized, primarily through maintaining good co-parenting relations. Children can literally be destroyed by fighting between parents, so it is very important that parents be able to work together for the well-being of their children. When not resolved, conflict can go on for years after the legal divorce is over. Children must be free of the feeling that loving one parent is a betrayal of the other. They must be free of the thought that they are the cause of the divorce.

Trying to create the ideal divorce is like any other ideal you try to achieve, like ideal health or achievement in some sport. Your goals are something you work toward, but you don't want to beat yourself up every time you fall short. Just try your best. The closer you can get, the better and smoother your divorce will go, and the better your future will be.

B. Creating order from chaos

Of course you should live your life whatever way seems best for you, but whenever you feel things are chaotic, overwhelming, out of hand and you don't know what else to do, try this approach.

In a nutshell, you make a list of all problems and organize them in order of immediacy and importance. Then you think about possible solutions for each item, dealing with the most pressing problems first. Keep working over the list and rearranging the items, but pay most attention to items at the top and try to do something about each one. Even emotional and life problems can be organized this way, but the easiest to pinpoint will be legal and practical. Use the worksheets that come on the companion CD to structure that part and you'll be way ahead. This method helps you see exactly what you have to deal with and it makes the unknown take shape and become manageable.

First things first. The order in which you want to solve problems will tend to follow the hierarchy developed by psychologist Abraham Maslow. He said that people have to satisfy their needs in this order, from primary physiological needs to higher aspirations of self and other:

Trying to create the ideal divorce is like any other ideal you try to achieve, like ideal health or achievement in some sport. Just try your best.

- Physiological needs—hunger, thirst, fatigue.
- Safety—shelter, avoidance of pain and anxiety, general physical security.
- Need to belong and feel loved—affection, intimacy, family and friends.
- Esteem—need for self-respect, a sense of competence.
- Self-actualization—to be fully what you can be; to explore knowledge, curiosity, aesthetics.

When a more primary need is unsatisfied, he said, all behavior tends to be directed to fulfilling it. If satisfaction is a recurring or continual problem, the higher levels will fail to develop properly. You can use Maslow's hierarchy to help guide the priority of items on your list of problems to solve.

For example, when hurt, any dumb animal knows enough to crawl into a den or a nest and lay still. People are smarter (so they say) but we don't always know enough to hole-up, get quiet and heal. Divorce can cause deep physical and emotional injury, so in the early stages the most important thing you can do at first is to create temporary physical safety and security for you and children in your custody. You need a place where, for a while, you can feel safe and a period of time to be relatively quiet, free of avoidable pressure and distraction.

When you feel relatively clear and ready to start dealing with your life, start a list of the problems you want to solve, like this:

- Write your thoughts on index cards as you read through this book, one subject per card. Rework your list as your understanding improves.

- Use one card for each problem and make notes on additional information you need to get and resources you can use to help in the solution.

Divorce can cause deep physical and emotional injury, so in the early stages the most important thing you can do at first is to create temporary physical safety and security for you and children in your custody.

- Keep reorganizing the items in order of priority. Put your most urgent and most important problems at the top.

- Write down your ideas for possible solutions. Talk to friends and family. Get ideas for solutions from this book, check out local family services and divorce support groups, or seek advice from professionals.

- In early days, don't try for a final solution for everything— look, instead, for short-term and temporary solutions whenever possible. Don't do any long-term planning until your life settles down and you can see more clearly. Be sure to take frequent time off from problem solving so you can relax.

- Now balance the problem list with a list of resources you can use and things you have to be grateful for. Write down your material and personal resources: assets, friends, family, health, job, and so on. Concentrate on your strengths: curiosity, love of life and people, your desire to grow and improve.

The important thing about upset is not if you are going to have it but how you are going to go through it.

Soon, you will see what you have to deal with. The whole confusing mess will have turned itself into a relatively short list of problems and each will have a variety of possible solutions. You may not be able to solve every problem—few people can—but you will know that you are doing your best with what you've got.

C. From grief to growth

In scientific studies of life's most stressful events, divorce always comes in at the very top. Those who leave have different emotions from those who get left, but the degree of turmoil is about the same. The important thing about upset is not if you are going to have it but how you are going to go through it.

How you go through your divorce is an expression of who you are. The way you deal with your problems will also determine who you will be when the divorce is long over and done with. "As the twig is bent, so grows the tree." You are creating your own future with every thought, word, and act.

Upset in divorce may range from mild to violent; it can feel like you've been physically torn—major surgery without anesthetic—or hit in the head, or just simply gone mad. Upset may last for weeks or months, even years. *You can't rush things,* but you *can* avoid getting stuck in the common traps discussed below.

Your experience is unique—no two divorces are the same, but most people experience the same four stages. This is how human beings are built:

1. **Shock.** The first two stages can be so intense and disorienting that you feel insane, wondering if you can cope. Yet everything happens at once and you have no choice—you must cope, and you will. You might experience symptoms of shock, like pain, numbness, feeling out of control or going crazy, loss of concentration, insomnia, extreme eating patterns. You might have wide swings in emotions. Intense anxiety, panic, anger, rage, depression can alternate with interludes of clarity, elation, optimism—and then back again. The shock stage can last from days to several months. It can be frightening and painful but it is *absolutely natural.*

   The danger at this stage is getting stuck in denial and numbness, turning your effort to avoid pain and anxiety into a way of life. You *have* to feel, you *have* to grieve and hurt. Don't escape into drink or drugs; just let it happen. Trying to deny or avoid or run from the experience will only make it last longer. The depth of your pain is also the measure of your capacity for love and joy.

2. **Roller coaster.** After the shock stage, the intensity tends to subside, perhaps become intermittent—this is the main difference from the shock stage—but you get confusing swings in emotions, especially your feelings for your mate and for yourself. You feel like you can't trust your feelings. Almost any little thing can set you off—a smell, a song, a memory. You dwell on the past, constantly reliving it and reevaluating. You might feel guilt, blame, self-blame, anger, shame, loss, loneliness, or depression. The way you think about yourself is shaky and uncertain; you feel incompetent, awkward, inadequate, unlovable. Your feelings go around and around and around; they seem to never settle down.

This is all natural, part of the grieving process, part of letting go of the past, and very necessary. It can go on for a few months to a year. You are under high stress and might be prone to illness and accident, so you have to take extra good care of yourself. Divorce is very much like recovering from major surgery. A big piece of your life has been removed. Be patient, be kind, pamper yourself a little.

You want to avoid getting stuck. Your feelings are valid, but don't make a career of them.

Your judgment is likely to be poor while in this state, so try to avoid making important decisions. Unfortunately, this is exactly when you have to deal with your divorce and create new arrangements for yourself and your children. Put off making permanent decisions if possible; try instead for temporary solutions. Whenever decisions are necessary, try to make them during calm interludes. Try not to be impulsive. If in doubt, consult trusted family and friends or stick to established standards such as those set by law. The middle of the road is safest on dark streets.

You want to avoid getting stuck. Your feelings are valid, but don't make a career of them. If you've been going around and around on the same themes, you will eventually have to stop spinning your wheels. If you dwell on loss, blame, or being wronged, you will prolong your own depression, anger, or fear. Don't get stuck too long—you need to get on with your life. Get out of your past and into your future.

3. **Self-development.** Your divorce is over when the end becomes a beginning. The roller coaster eventually evens out more and more. Now you begin to notice the possibilities of your new life. The present and the future become more important than the past. You pay a lot of attention to yourself and your image. You make plans. You make new friends, experiment with new interests and experiences. You may act like a kid again. Dating and sex may bring on a certain degree of confusion, a rerun of old feelings from as far back as adolescence. Have fun discovering what you are, who you are and who you like—but don't overdo it.

Your divorce is over when the end becomes a beginning.

4. **Emergence.** You are getting comfortable with yourself, getting stronger, increasingly clear and aware of who you are. You are more interested in the present and the future. You have a new center of balance as a single person, whole and complete to yourself, and you are now ready for intimacy in new relationships. You survived the divorce and have been strengthened by it. You can still feel grief and sadness about the past, but without guilt, blame or resentment. You are no longer threatened by your own feelings.

Your spouse is going through these cycles, too. Whatever anger and grief your spouse is experiencing is helping to break the bonds of attachment. It is a necessary part of the healing process.

Components of the emotional cycle

Pain. You have to recognize that pain is not only natural, it can be a helper and a good adviser. Especially at first, pain may only mean that you have been injured and are healing, as if you had broken your leg or suffered a serious wound. But at other times it can be a message that something is wrong, that you have to pay attention to something you have been ignoring. The intensity of pain during divorce can be frightening, but you must not run from it or try to block it out or avoid it. To do so will delay your healing or even leave you permanently impaired in spirit. Instead, embrace it; let it happen. The pain is in your heart space and that is where the real "you" lives, so it is calling you home to your center and to your real self. Endure your suffering, accept your pain and listen to it. If you do, it will run its course and you will heal more quickly; it will lead you to your solutions; it will provide the energy for your changes and growth; it will make you stronger.

Fear. The major challenge in any divorce is to deal constructively with fear. Fear of pain, fear of hurt, fear of the future, fear of your ability to take care of yourself and your children, fear of losing self-respect, fear of fear. There is a basic bewilderment of life when so much is happening that you feel you can't cope; you just don't know what to do or how to live. Fear is the root source of anger. Anger is the flip-side of fear. Anger turned inward is depression.

Anger is a potent source of energy and a very useful emotion—if you know how to use it.

Anger. Learning how to use anger constructively is one of the most important lessons to be gained from your divorce. Anger is a potent source of energy and a very useful emotion—if you know how to use it. Anger helps you get through the first and most painful stages by providing an outlet for inexpressible emotions and it helps break the bonds of affection and attachment.

For people who have never shown it, learning how to get angry is a big step forward. Anger will help you stop being dependent, stop being a victim. Anger and action are better than making a career of being depressed, downtrodden, and helpless. You *can* learn to be angry, assertive and constructive all at the same time.

On the other hand, some people become addicted to anger and they misuse it badly. Anger soon becomes self-defeating and self-destructive; the cause of bad mistakes in judgment (like running to a lawyer before you are prepared) that will work against your own interests. Anger can drag you into an uncontrolled battle.

The attraction of anger is that it is cheap and easy—easier than actually solving real problems; easier than taking responsibility for your own life. It is reliable, always there; you can count on it. For just a moment, it gives you a false sense of power and control; it lets off your steam. But anger is a solution that solves nothing. It serves only to distract you from having to face your own pain, fear or guilt. If you abuse anger, if you become a habitual user, it will poison your life and turn you into an unhealthy, lonely, bitter, spiteful person. You can count on it.

Someone can hurt you only if you give them the power to do so.

For cases with extreme conflict, read section F below and chapter 9.

Hurt. It is a painful and terrible thing to be hurt by someone you depend on, someone you loved and trusted. In the early stages of divorce, you might need to heal from hurt, but you do not need to continue allowing yourself to be hurt. Someone can hurt you only if you give them the power to do so. Hurt then becomes something that you do to yourself, something you permit to happen. To paraphrase an old Scottish saying, "Hurt me once, shame on you! Hurt me twice, shame on me!" Staying hurt long after the divorce is over keeps you stuck on your needs and weaknesses; it reinforces your picture of yourself as a victim.

D. Healing

Healing starts with a lot of tiny changes in your daily habits. If you take charge of the little things, the big ones will soon fall in line. You should see it as a triumph when you learn to do for yourself the little things that you always depended on your spouse to do, or make decisions in areas where you always used to defer to your mate. Take pleasure in your new self-reliance when you learn to cook, take care of business, grow house plants, remember birthdays, mow the lawn, create an enjoyable living space, or keep the checkbook balanced. When you change your daily habits in the small ways, you are on your way up.

One of your great healing strengths is whatever it is that got you this far in this book—your curiosity, your desire to know things, a desire to take control of your life. Think about your other strengths and advantages.

Gratitude. Another major healing force—one of the most important—is gratitude. This is something you can work on intentionally. Focus on the things in your life that are right at least as much and as often as you dwell on problems. Several times each day, take the time to get quiet inside yourself and think about all the things that you have to be grateful for. Make a list; try to develop a strong sense of gratitude for your life and its many blessings.

Take responsibility for your own feelings, for your own life.

Self-reliance. Getting divorced means that you will no longer let your mate's moods and actions dominate your life. You are disentangling yourself from all the old patterns that didn't work for you. You can't control your spouse, but you can start to control your own actions. Learn not to react to your spouse's bad conduct and not to push back when your own buttons get pushed. Take responsibility for your own feelings, for your own life.

Acceptance and forgiveness. Possibly the most effective way to speed the healing process—the best way to achieve your own health and balance—is to completely accept your loss, feel your pain, and try to forgive your ex-mate and yourself. Guilt and blame are heavy burdens that can only hold you back and drag you down. Not forgiving keeps you stuck in a view of yourself as a victim. For your own sake, let it all go. Letting go is very different from repressing. You can't heal properly if you deny, avoid or repress your feelings—to the contrary, you want to feel your pain and loss.

If you accept your feelings, they will run a natural, healing course; then you can forgive, let go of the past and get on with your life.

Support. Make an effort to seek out and use the help and comfort that is available from people in your life. You need the support of friends and family. If you can get it, use it. You can also get a lot of help from family services organizations, divorce support groups and single parent support groups. Make the effort to contact them; it might be useful and you have nothing to lose. For references, call your local social services or human resources agency or the local courthouse clerks. You can also get references to support groups in your area through a local church or temple. If one group isn't what you want, try another. Then, there's the professional support that you can get from working with a good counselor. Chapter 7E discusses how to choose a counselor.

Make an effort to seek out and use the help and comfort that is available from people in your life.

In divorce, your emotional problems (looking backward) often disguise a great opportunity (looking forward). As Nietzsche said, taking a hard line, "That which does not kill us makes us strong." Another way to look at it is that you can learn what is really important in life and what your goals really are. At the very least, you can learn not to create the same old patterns, not to repeat the same mistakes.

E. Psychological traps

Pain is natural and unavoidable when you separate, but people have many ways of unwittingly increasing their pain and prolonging it. A lot of your pain might be entirely unnecessary.

Most unnecessary pain is caused by a very bad habit—negative thinking. There are self-defeating thought patterns that keep you stuck in anger, anxiety or depression. Although they are usually not aware of it, most people almost continually describe the world to themselves, and it's that quiet, constant voice that forms your attitude—your predisposition to experience things negatively. Don't be too quick to decide that you don't do this—it is so habitual that you might not be aware of it. That's what makes it hard to cope with.

Negative thinking causes you to paint your life in black with too broad a brush. The way you see things will be one-sided, overly simple and unbalanced. Negative thinking keeps you boxed in, limits your possibilities, keeps you from seeing solutions and prevents you from moving forward with your life. What you think turns into what you feel. If you expect the worst, that might be what you get. Here are some classic examples of negative thinking:

- **Over-generalizing** is when you think or say things like, "You always put me down," or "I'll never find another mate," or "She only wants one thing from me." You have picked on one negative feature and made it into your total understanding. Try to stop using words like all, always, every, never, only, and totally.

- **Labeling** would be, "He's a selfish person," or "She's a bitch," or "I'm a loser." You pick on one negative quality and let that represent the whole person. This keeps you angry at others and disgusted with yourself.

- **Blame** of self or others makes it seem as if the fault for your misfortune is all one-sided, but life is never like that and blame has unfortunate side-effects. If you blame yourself, you are trapped in guilt. If you blame your spouse, you make yourself a victim, avoid your own responsibility, and prolong your anger. That's all over now; the fact is that you each made your own choices and are responsible for your own actions. Now, get on with your life.

Negative thinking keeps you boxed in, limits your possibilities, keeps you from seeing solutions and prevents you from moving forward with your life.

- **Filtering** happens when you see only the negative or threatening side of things. Focusing on fears and losses will keep you locked in anxiety or depression.

- **Catastrophizing** is when you exaggerate potential threats and stay focused on *anticipated* harm or disaster. "I'll never be able to pay my bills." "I can't survive this pain and loneliness." You expect the worst and don't expect to cope.

To avoid the consequences of negative thinking, you have to become more aware of your inner voices and attitudes. Try to notice when you are scaring yourself or seeing things through an all-black filter. When you catch yourself at it, stop. When the negative thoughts start again (and they will), catch them again. Keep at it. Don't be self-critical and put yourself down; just observe and be patient. Give yourself a little reward each time you catch yourself—a cookie or a balloon. Don't laugh, it works. Make yourself think in a more constructive vein: concentrate on solutions instead of problems, think about past pleasures, fantasize about future ones. Try to make yourself take a more balanced and rounded view of things. Stop and breathe, take a walk. Go get some flowers, make your space nice. Keep your attention focused only on things you can see, touch or smell.

Reducing conflict never means that you have to compromise your rights or self-respect.

This is hard work and it takes a long time. Don't put yourself down if you don't succeed overnight. A good counselor can help a lot with this kind of work.

F. How to reduce conflict and stress

Reducing conflict never means that you have to compromise your rights or self-respect. It can be hard work, but making the effort can help personally, whether or not it reaches your spouse or gets you an agreement. Those are by-products; the real benefit is inside.

Conflict is what happens when two people have a different way of looking at the same facts or develop different goals and interests. It happens all the time; so what?

- Healthy conflict leads to solutions. It's not always easy, but you can usually work things out through discussion and compromise.

- Unhealthy conflict is when negative emotions pervert or displace an otherwise honest disagreement. The emotions that fuel unhealthy conflict are a combination of each spouse's own ancient attitudes, experiences, and habits coupled with all the patterns and distortions built up in the relationship. Untangling any part of this terrible can of worms will be a blessing for the rest of your life.

Insecure, upset spouses

You can't negotiate with someone who is insecure, upset, or fearful. If pressed, they are likely to retain a lawyer to fight for them.

If your spouse is insecure (and not a habitual conroller/abuser), there's a lot you can do to help. Let your spouse know you'll be open and fair and make no moves without letting him/her know ahead of time. Make sure both sides have some stability for the time it takes to settle things. Tone yourself back, listen more, don't argue, repeat yourself, or insist. Take it slow and easy and help your spouse gain the confidence to negotiate. Do not try to con your spouse because if he/she catches on, you'll have lost trust for the rest of your miserable and expensive lawsuit. If lawyers get into it, the con could come back to haunt you years later.

Let your spouse know you'll be open and fair and make no moves without letting him/her know ahead of time.

If you are the insecure person, you have to get some backbone or get help. You'll feel a lot better if you get informed and prepared by following the steps in this book. You'll probably get some advice and learn for certain what you have a right to. You'll come to grips with the financial aspects of life that you let someone else take care of before. This is the new you. If you feel you just can't go through this alone and want someone to represent you, look for a collaborative lawyer near you (chapter 7) and encourage your spouse to get one, too.

Breaking old patterns

The divorce starts to work for you when you learn to untangle yourself from those ugly dances you used to do.

Most couples, not just those in trouble, have a predictable pattern of interaction that doesn't work. You have your own set of triggers that set you off more or less the same way every time, over and over. You have habits for dealing with disagreements that do not serve you well or solve problems. It may not be intentional, it may not be conscious, but you know each other's buttons and you push them automatically without thinking, especially when feeling angry, frightened or guilty.

Don't do that anymore.

Maybe it doesn't take much of a push on a button to get your bell to ring; maybe you are so upset that it rings almost by itself. Maybe your spouse is in a highly emotional condition too, acting like someone you wish you never knew and you are taking it all very personally. Don't do that either.

Stop letting your mate's moods dominate your life. That's over. You are not divorcing just your spouse, you are also divorcing yourself from all those old patterns that didn't work. The divorce starts to work for you when you learn to untangle yourself from those ugly dances you used to do. If you could stop (easier said than done), your mate might keep on for a while but will eventually have to notice that it's a solo performance. If not, too bad, but your ex-mate's problems aren't yours. Your problem is how you act, how you feel, and how to handle your own life.

Curiosity is a great attitude and a great tool. The most constructive thing you can do is to try to observe and discover the mutual patterns that never did and still don't work. More particularly, you want to understand the part you play. Don't try to change anything, not at first; just observe when it's happening. Stop. Breathe. Even if you don't untangle the web, taking this attitude will be a big improvement.

You probably can't control your mate, but you can concentrate on healing your own emotions and controlling your own actions. This is about controlling actions, not feelings. Don't try to control your feelings — they are real and valid. Observe your feelings, accept them, but express them some other way.

Honest, open listening is the best thing you can do when someone is angry.

Dealing with anger

Even while an event is in progress, you can be trying to figure out what the anger is all about. Anger is the flip-side of fear. When someone is afraid, the least little thing will set them off into a crisis of reactive anger. Fear is mostly unconscious and usually about not having enough: not enough security, power, respect, love or stability. Fear is about loss of face, not being in control, not having enough money, fear of change, fear of responsibility, things like that. What is your spouse afraid of? What are you afraid of?

To figure out what anger is about, you have to listen. Honest, open listening is the best thing you can do when someone is angry. You don't have to buy into their anger or agree with their point-of-view, just understand. If you are sincerely trying to hear what the angry person is saying and understand what's behind the anger—if you are not reacting to it, defending yourself from it, arguing, denying, dismissing or patronizing—then their anger will have nothing to feed on and will spend itself sooner. The angry person may save face by staying huffy and self-righteous, but your attitude will be noticed and will have a cumulative effect over time. If not fed, anger collapses from its own weight.

Working on yourself

Working on yourself is the most interesting of all possible tasks. It may be the hardest—and most rewarding—thing you will ever do. This is when you develop your sense of personal responsibility. You are breaking your psychological dependency on your spouse, no longer depending on your mate for your own sense of well-being and worth; you will no longer let your feelings be determined by your mate's moods and actions.

You and only you are responsible for your feelings and your actions.

You and only you are responsible for your feelings and your actions. It isn't your fault when you are down, or anyone else's, but it is your responsibility to get up.

When times are hard, pay special attention to your body. Take care of it; relax it; be good to it. This is a healing time. Eat well, get healthy. Slow down, be quiet, hole up, nest. Get a massage, work on those knots. Take hot baths and/or cold showers, whatever works. Feeling bad isn't so bad if you don't feel bad about it. Just let it happen; it's proof you're alive and learning.

You know how sometimes it's easy for you to see what's really going on between two arguing people? Or how you can observe other people's patterns when they can't? What if someone could do that for you now? This is a good time to get some third person to listen, observe, give you feedback and advice. That's what professional family counselors are trained to do. Counseling and how to choose a counselor are discussed in chapter 7E.

Friends are wonderful moral support, but don't take advice from just anybody. Listen only to people who have wisdom and experience. Being a friend and caring about you doesn't make that person qualified to give good advice. If your friend is helping you get worked up, dwell on grievances or wallow in your stuff, get your advice somewhere else.

Practical Pointers

1. Anger is not reasonable. When someone reaches the flash point, the ability to reason gets less as anger increases. Don't bother trying to talk sense until the anger is well past. Anger always passes. It runs its course faster if you don't feed it, faster yet if you use defusing techniques (below).

2. Deal with the problem, not the person.

3. You do not have to give in or be a doormat.

    - **Rights.** You have the right to act in your own best interest; to respect and stand up for yourself; to politely express ideas and honest emotions; to ask for what you want; to set limits; to be treated with respect and dignity; to make mistakes and accept responsibility.

    - **Responsibilities.** It is your responsibility to respect and honor the same rights for your mate; to take responsibility for your own behavior.

Your goal is to keep things calm so you can deal with the problem or complete the business at hand.

4. Be assertive and constructive:

    - Confront the problem, not the person.

    - Defuse the hostility, don't play at patterns that don't work. Your goal is to keep things calm so you can deal with the problem or complete the business at hand.

    - Disengage from the conflict. Pay attention to your

own anger level; when necessary, express your need to interrupt the cycle and allow a cool-down period. Reschedule another time to work on the problem, then get up and quietly leave.

5. **Defusing.** Here are some techniques for defusing anger when it comes up:

    *   Remain calm yourself. Don't react—instead, use your sense of curiosity; become an interested observer. Encourage talking by listening openly.

    *   Show that you understand or are trying to. Nod, paraphrase and mirror what you hear ("Let's see if I have this right; you are saying that _____?"). You must be sincere in this for it to work well.

    *   Talk to your spouse with "I" messages instead of the accusing "you." For example, "I can't discuss this when the TV is on so loud," instead of "You are noisy and totally inconsiderate."

    *   Make statements about yourself when necessary, but not about your mate personally. Be specific and concrete, be positive not negative.

    *   Calmly set your limits. "If you keep yelling, I am going to leave," or "If you are more than 30 minutes late picking up the children, I will have to leave with them."

    *   Don't defend or attack, don't generalize ("You always do this to me"), don't be sarcastic or discuss your mate's motives or dig up old history.

Talk to your spouse with "I" messages instead of the accusing "you."

- Deal with the specific matter now at hand.

- Reassure your mate; help him or her to save face.

- Remember, your goal is to reach agreement, not score points.

6. Work with the attitude that you want to find solutions that allow you both to get what you want and need. Avoid the win/lose attitude.

7. Don't expect a quick fix or miracles. You can do all the right things and not have immediate results. It's like erosion, the sort of thing you have to chip away at. It takes time, but you will succeed if you keep at it.

G. Rules of the road for getting through a tough time

Break old patterns that don't work; learn new ones that do.

The important thing is to make up your own mind and take charge of your own life. You can't control anyone else, certainly not your spouse, but you do have control over your own thoughts, actions, and responses. Start working there. Break old patterns that don't work; learn new ones that do.

You have to do the inner work yourself. You can get help from professionals or friends or books, but in the final analysis you have to look inside for answers to life's problems. Whether you discover your own answers or borrow the best advice you can find from wherever you can find it, the choice—and the task—is yours.

Here, on the next pages, are some rules of the road for the divorce journey. These are adapted from material developed by Sharon Baker for use in her family counseling practice in Rancho Palos Verdes, California.

RULES OF THE ROAD #1
Getting yourself through a tough time

1. You can expect to go through cycles of:

   - Shock and denial
   - Anger/depression
   - Understanding and acceptance

   Then you go around and around many times between anger or depression and acceptance. After a time, acceptance becomes stronger and lasts longer.

2. Let your attention focus on your loss, a good way to understand your pain. There is a message in your pain that will lead to solutions. Pain can give you motivation and energy to bring about changes.

3. Seek quiet and rest. Take extra good care of yourself. Exercise, eat properly, keep life as simple as possible.

4. Acknowledge and express your feelings. Talk to someone who knows how to listen. Keep a journal.

5. Seek out support from friends, family, clergy, divorce or crisis support groups, counselors.

6. Stay aware. Do not try to alter or numb your feelings with substances, such as alcohol, drugs, or overeating.

7. Be realistic in what you expect from yourself. It is normal to have mood changes, to feel confused, to have mixed feelings about your spouse.

8. Have faith in your beliefs and in yourself. Remember to be grateful for what you do have. Having life, you are a miracle of creation. You are alive, you can feel, you can learn, you can grow.

9. Work. Enjoy the benefits of a daily schedule and of accomplishment, especially in the small changes you are gradually adding to your life to make it better.

10. Be good to yourself.

11. Take time to be with adults and, when you are ready, go out and enjoy social activities.

12. Remember that healing is already in process. Time and nature are on your side. You will recover!

RULES OF THE ROAD #2
Getting children through a tough time

1. Tell children the truth in simple terms with simple explanations. Tell them where their other parent has gone.

2. Reassure them that they will continue to be taken care of and that they will be safe and secure.

3. Your children will see that parents can stop loving each other, stop getting along, stop living together. Reassure them that a parent's love for a child is a special kind that never stops.

4. Spend time with each child individually. Whether you have custody or visitation, the most important thing to the child is your individual relationship. Build the best relationship you can in your circumstances. The future is built of many tiny moments.

5. Children may feel responsible for causing the divorce. Reassure them that they are not to blame. They may also feel that it is their responsibility to bring their parents back together. Let them know that your decision is final and will have to be accepted.

6. Divorcing parents often feel guilty and become overindulgent. Give your child love, but set limits. Children thrive within reasonable limits.

7. Your child is still a child and can't become the man of the house or a little mother. Continue to be a parent to your child. Seek other adults to fill your own need for companionship.

8. Avoid situations that place a child in the impossible position of choosing between parents:

   • Don't use your child as a way to get back at your spouse. Children can be terribly wounded when caught in a cross-fire.

   • Don't say bad things about the other parent in hearing of a child.

   • Don't say or do anything that might discourage the child from spending time with the other parent.

   • Don't encourage a child to take sides.

9. You are both the parents of your children for life. Pledge to cooperate responsibly and reasonably toward their growth and development as an expression of your mutual love for them.

10. Be patient and understanding with your children. Be patient and understanding with yourself.

4

TIPS ON DIVORCE LAW
– Property, support and parenting

THE LEGAL DIVORCE has very limited concerns. To get divorced, you have to make decisions about your property, children, and support. That's it. That's all the legal divorce is about, unless you have a high degree of conflict, in which case it is also about keeping the peace and protecting you, your children and your property.

What you get from your legal divorce is a piece of paper—a judgment or decree—with findings of fact and court orders on the above subjects. That's all. This is what all the fuss is about. This is what people go to attorneys for and spend tens or hundreds of thousands of dollars to get—a piece of paper with orders about peace, property, custody, and support.

Obviously, these are important subjects and you need to deal with them anyway. But there are many ways to settle these matters and, in almost all cases, the legal process is very low on the list of recommended methods. You might think that a legal divorce will solve your problems, but it probably won't and it is critically important that you understand this so you don't expect too much from the legal divorce and set yourself up for frustration and disappointment.

To get divorced, you have to make decisions about your property, children, and support. That's it.

Laws are for judges. The law must be followed by judges when a disagreement has been taken to court. Outside of court, you can agree to almost anything (within reason) that seems fair to you without much reference to laws. Where children are concerned, however, a judge might review your terms to make sure the children are reasonably well supported and protected. Terms that are grossly unfair are vulnerable to attack later if the disadvantaged spouse regrets the agreement.

Once you understand exactly what the legal divorce is about, you can focus on organizing your facts, negotiating with your spouse and making decisions. As you begin to sort out your new life and your current problems, it is important to know what help you can get from the law and which problems you will have to solve yourself in some other way. Unfortunately, people often get so wrapped up in the legal divorce that they lose sight of their real-life goals and solutions. While a legal divorce is not exactly useless, never forget that your best and most effective solutions involve personal changes and practical, day-to-day actions that take place outside of the context of laws, lawyers and courts.

Your legal divorce is over when you get your judgment, but your real divorce is not over until you have your self back; when pain, anger, hurt, blame, and guilt are finished; when your ex-spouse no longer has the power to push your buttons; when you are comfortable in the middle of your own life as a single person. This can happen very soon, many years from now, or never, but this is the real goal of your divorce.

After all we have said to show the limitations of the legal divorce, it may seem contradictory that most of this book is devoted to helping you get through it. But the fact is, to get divorced, you have to go through the legal divorce, and you must settle the issues that the law cares most about. The purpose of this book is to help you get through the legal divorce without getting caught up in its traps and harmed by a system that works so badly.

While a legal divorce is not exactly useless, never forget that your best and most effective solutions involve personal changes and practical, day-to-day actions that take place outside of the context of laws, lawyers and courts.

A. Keeping the peace

In cases with high conflict, you can get court orders to keep the peace and protect yourself, your children or your property. For example, ordering one spouse not to contact, annoy or harass the other; or to move out of the house; or not to encumber or transfer any property except in the usual course of business or for necessities (like your divorce attorney); or not to cancel or transfer any insurance held for the benefit of either the other spouse or a child.

If there are children, orders can be made forbidding the removal of a child of the parties from the state without written permission of the other spouse or consent of the court, or for visitation away from the family premises or, if necessary, through a third person.

Restraining orders will often help control a bad situation. They are effective in about 85% of all cases. But you also have to find ways to help yourself. Your own attitude and your determination to change things is actually the most important ingredient in any solution. Self-help includes learning new response patterns, joining a support group, calling on friends, clergy or the police for help, moving away, hiding, taking karate classes, and so on.

Your own attitude and your determination to change things is actually the most important ingredient in any solution.

B. Dissolving the bonds

There are three ways to end a marriage:

- Divorce (or dissolution),
- Legal separation (or separate maintenance), and
- Annulment (or nullity).

Separation gets you the same orders for peace, property, custody and support as a divorce, but the parties stay married. Some people have moral or religious reasons for not wanting a divorce, and sometimes there is an economic reason—such as where there are sizable retirement, Social Security or veteran's benefits to be lost in case of divorce, or where one spouse is covered under the other spouse's health insurance program and has a health problem that would cause a hardship if the coverage were lost.

An annulment declares that the marriage never existed at all, because the marriage was illegal at the outset or founded on fraud.

You can't stop a divorce. If only one spouse wants a divorce and the other resists, there will be a divorce. At best you can slow things down a bit and make it more costly, but the most you will get is a contest on the terms of property, custody or support. One of the major traps in the legal divorce—the thing that leads to a lot of unnecessary expense and conflict—is that people get so emotionally upset about breaking up that they fight over anything that can be fought over, fighting on the wrong issues for the wrong reasons. But the divorce goes through anyway.

You can't stop a divorce. If only one spouse wants a divorce and the other resists, there will be a divorce.

What follows is a checklist of things you want to clarify when you learn the rules that apply in your state (section F below):

Grounds. Almost all states have "no-fault" divorce. In these states, the court is not concerned at all with who is to blame for the marriage not working out—so there's no future in trying to untangle that can of worms—but only with the facts and circumstances of property, custody and support. Some states have grounds for divorce that involve fault and, unfortunately, a few states permit fault to influence awards of property and support, although this is becoming increasingly rare.

Residency. Most states have a residency requirement that must be satisfied before you can get a divorce—a minimum period of weeks or months that you must have lived in the state. Being away temporarily, as on business trips or vacations, is okay and does not count against your residency time. If one spouse is on active military duty, the divorce cannot be filed without that spouse's cooperation unless you go through complex legal procedures.

Waiting periods. Some states impose a waiting period, a minimum amount of time that must pass before the divorce can become effective. In a few states, the couple must have been living separately for a period of time before the divorce. These delays are supposed to give the couple a last chance to reconcile. It is always possible to get valid orders on the legal issues (peace, property, custody, support) earlier than the divorce date. Legal separation might have no waiting period or a different period from divorce.

Simplified procedures. Many states have procedures that are simplified for some divorces: those by agreement or for short-term marriages with no children and minimal property. Many states make it possible to complete a divorce without a court hearing. In most states, even if there is a hearing, it is mere routine.

C. Property, income and debts

If your estate is complex, you might need an accountant or some legal advice to help untangle it. If spouses disagree, don't hesitate to get several opinions. Where the law is not clear, try to settle disagreements according to personal values and understandings. Admit that there is room for a difference of opinion. Weigh the amount involved against the cost of a legal battle—it will almost always cost more to fight than to compromise.

Weigh the amount involved against the cost of a legal battle—it will almost always cost more to fight than to compromise.

Get organized and make decisions. In order to get through a legal divorce, you have to itemize, characterize, value, and divide all your property. The Assets and Debts Worksheet (on the CD) will help you do this. You will need to develop the following information:

- Itemize: what property do you own?
- Characterize: label each item as to whether it is subject

to division (acquired during marriage) or not subject to division (in most states, this is property acquired before marriage and, possibly, after separation). Learn the rules of property division for your state before you do this step.

- Value: how much is the property to be divided worth?
- Divide: how will it be divided?

1. **Itemize.** Make a list of everything of value you own. Small items can be grouped together under a general item heading, such as "jewelry," or "household goods," or "sports equipment."

2. **Characterize.** Label each item as whether or not it is separate or marital property and therefore subject to division in a divorce. To determine who owns what, you need to learn about the laws and how they apply to the facts in your case.

To determine who owns what, you need to learn about the laws and how they apply to the facts in your case.

3. **Value.** Establish the fair-market value of property that is to be divided. This is not what you paid for an item or what it is worth to you or what it will be worth someday. *Fair-market value* means what you would get if you sold the item on the open market on the date it is being divided. There is room for differences of opinion on value, so this is something you would like to work on with your spouse; at least communicate about it so your spouse doesn't think you are trying to be sly. Differences of opinion can be settled by a professional appraiser. Always get an appraisal for large or hard-to-value items, such as real property, pensions or a going business. You do not have to value property that will be divided in kind. For example, if each spouse takes an equal number of XYZ shares, it doesn't matter how much they are worth. If you agree to sell the house (or anything) on the open market and split the net proceeds, the fair value will be determined by the sale.

4. **Divide.** Separate (non-marital) property does not get divided because it already belongs to one person, but it is a very good idea to list and confirm the ownership of valuable or special items for the record and for the sake of clarity in the future. Marital property can be divided any way you like by agreement. If you can't agree, it will be divided in court by a judge according to the rules of your state. You want to learn and understand those rules, but you are especially interested in how predictable they are; that is, can you predict with fair accuracy what a judge would do if presented with the facts of your case? Try very hard to reach agreement through negotiation or mediation, because a legal battle over property will almost always cost more than you can gain by fighting over it. If all else fails, consider binding arbitration; it's cheaper.

Before deciding how to divide any major item of property, it is essential that you understand the tax consequences of changes in title. Read more about this in the section on taxes, below, and maybe get advice from a tax accountant.

Deciding what to do with a family home is both an emotional and a financial decision.

The family home and other real estate

The value of what you own in real estate, or any other property, is called your "equity"—the amount you can actually sell it for on the open market less all amounts owing on it and less the cost of sale. This is the amount that is being divided.

Deciding what to do with a family home is both an emotional and a financial decision. If the home is otherwise a sound investment, and if you figured in the cost of maintenance, taxes and insurance, owning it can mean security and stability. If you have children, it could be better if they stay in a house, neighborhood and school system they are used to. But, on the other hand, it might be full of memories and ghosts of the past, so it could be bad for you emotionally. If you can't afford to keep the house, or if you need cash more than security and stability, you could sell the house, move to a more modest accommodation, and invest the money you have saved. Will your decision lock you into your past or will it represent a sound financial investment? Do you need money or stability? You get to decide.

Don't forget to look into tax consequences before you make any decision regarding the family home. A spouse who takes property or money for a share of the home as part of a divorce settlement has no tax liability from that trade. A spouse who keeps title to the house also keeps the tax basis of the house and future liability for capital gains, if any. If the house is to be sold and proceeds divided later, some time after the divorce, then a spouse who has moved out of the house will (unless it was done very, very carefully) no longer be able to claim the house as a personal residence and may therefore have lost the right to postpone capital gains taxes with a "rollover."

Don't forget to look into tax consequences before you make any decision regarding the family home.

Contact your local IRS office and get a current copy of the free IRS publication number 523, *Selling Your Home*.

Ten ways to divide property without a fight

This list was originally developed by Judge Robert K. Garth of Riverside, California as an aid to spouses having trouble reaching agreement about the division of their property.

1. **Barter.** Each party takes certain items of property in exchange for other items. For instance, the car and furniture in exchange for the truck and tools.

2. **Choose items alternately.** The spouses take turns selecting items from a list of all the marital property, without regard for the value of items selected.

3. **One spouse divides, the other chooses**. One spouse divides all the marital property into two parts and the other spouse gets the choice of parts.

4. **One spouse values, the other chooses.** One spouse places a value on each item of marital property and the other spouse gets the choice of items up to an agreed share of the total value.

5. **Appraisal and alternate selection.** A third person (such as an appraiser) agreed upon by the parties places a value on contested items of marital property and the parties choose alternately until one spouse has chosen items worth his or her share of the marital property.

6. **Sale.** Some or all of the marital property is sold and the proceeds divided.

7. **Secret bids.** The spouses place secret bids on each item of marital property and the one who bids highest for an item gets it. Where one receives items that exceed his or her share of the total value, there will be an equalization payment to the other spouse.

8. **Private auction.** The spouses openly bid against each other on each item of marital property. If one spouse gets more than their share, an equalization payment can be made.

9. **Arbitration.** The spouses select an arbitrator who will decide the matter of valuation and division after hearing from both spouses and considering all evidence.

10. **Mediation.** The spouses select a mediator who works to help them reach an agreement on the matters of valuation and division.

Inform your spouse before you close accounts or do anythng that will affect him or her.

Income and debts

Learn how income and debts are treated in your state. Does income after separation belong to both spouses or the one who earns it? What about retirement benefits or any form of delayed income earned, at least in part, during your marriage?

Learn the rules about who is responsible for debts incurred before, during and after marriage, in one name or both names. It is very important for you to close or remove your name from all joint accounts and credit cards and give written notice to creditors that you ever dealt with as a couple, saying that you will no longer be responsible for debts of your spouse. Inform your spouse before you close accounts or do anything that will affect him or her.

You will always be liable for any debt for which you were liable when it was originally incurred.

You will always be liable for any debt for which you were liable when it was originally incurred. Orders of the court and agreements between spouses about who must pay particular debts are only effective between the spouses and do not affect the creditors. If your spouse doesn't pay such a debt, you are still obligated. This is why many settlement agreements have a clause that requires one spouse to notify the other if ever they go bankrupt on debts acquired during the marriage.

The following is a practical scheme for dividing debts that might help you make decisions. It's not based on any law but on the practical idea that debts should go to the person most likely to pay them. If this scheme leads you to an unfair property division, consider an equalization payment—or a note if it can be secured with other property—to make things come out right.

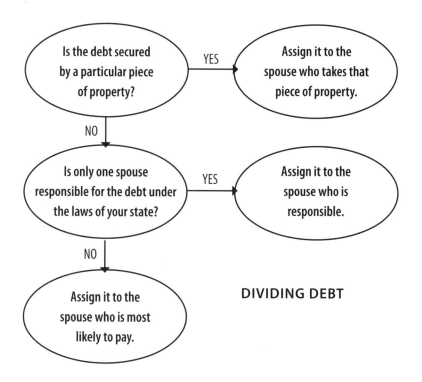

DIVIDING DEBT

D. Parenting plans (custody and visitation)

If you have children, you need a parenting plan—a schedule for the future care of your children. Two sample plans are on the CD that comes with this book. This is an emotional issue, perhaps the most important matter you deal with. It is critically important that you resolve the parenting relationship with a minimum of bad feeling and a maximum of cooperation. Children need both of their parents and the parents need all the help they can get from each other in raising them. Harm to children from divorce is more closely related to conflict *after* the divorce so your goal is to make arrangements that both parents can live with agreeably. See the last pages of chapter 3 and chapter 6, step 2, on protecting your children. It is important to try to avoid anything that makes either parent feel he or she is "losing" the child to the other parent. A child is not an object to be won or lost.

Children need both of their parents and the parents need all the help they can get from each other in raising them.

Start communicating with your spouse to see what will work best for the children and still be comfortable for both of you. To help with the negotiation and planning of child custody matters, use the Parental Activity Worksheet on the CD. It will give you a realistic view of how child-rearing chores have been shared in the past and how you intend to share them in the future.

It might help if you learn how your local judges deal with child-related issues when parents can't agree. Unfortunately, the rules of law are generally useful only in court, after it's already too late.

Experience shows that pure joint custody—sharing parental rights and responsibility—works best for parents who are cooperative and capable of working out future problems as they come up. The widely used parenting plan provides for joint legal custody for both parents, primary residence (or physical custody) for one parent, and a schedule that shows in detail exactly when each parent will have custody of the child. This sort of arrangement provides stability while helping reduce the sense of alienation and loss of the out-parent. Finally, there is the old-fashioned sole-custody award of primary physical *and* legal custody to one parent with a visitation schedule for the other. This is used primarily where the parents are unlikely to be cooperative.

After judgment, parents can depart freely from their agreed plan from day to day by mutual agreement, but whenever they can't agree to something different, they can rely on what the plan says.

A detailed plan helps to create stability, security and settle any disagreements. After judgment, parents can depart freely from their agreed plan from day to day by mutual agreement, but whenever they can't agree to something different, they can rely on what the plan says. This is why the plan should be as detailed as possible. If the plan is sufficiently detailed, it doesn't matter as much what legal terms you use for the parenting relationship because the parents will know in any case where the child will be. See the sample parenting plans on the CD.

Mediation. If you can't agree on a parenting plan, the matter will have to be decided in court—a very expensive and destructive process. Before it gets that far, you should first try to settle it with the help of a professional mediator. Experience shows that a few sessions can be very effective, having about an 80% success rate. Many states *require* mediation of custody disagreements.

After the divorce, if co-parenting does not work well, you should consider professional couples-counseling to help you work better at co-parenting. You can also get a lot of help from the many parent support groups and family service agencies.

E. Child and spousal support

Support for children and spouses raises the fact that the same family income must now support two households. Obviously, some changes must be made and the spouse who didn't want the divorce will be most displeased. Here is yet another reason why it is essential to work for mutual acceptance of the divorce and agreement on terms. Support orders are often not paid in full and on time, but support that has been agreed to has a much higher rate of full and timely compliance.

Support orders are often not paid in full and on time, but support that has been agreed to has a much higher rate of full and timely compliance.

If child or spousal support will be an issue in your case, first get your financial information together using the worksheets on the CD that comes with this book, then learn the law in your state. The Budget Worksheet is very important to your financial planning, so don't let it slide—it is essential. If you have trouble with it, seek the help of a financial counselor. Look in the white pages for Consumer Credit Counselors, ask the Better Business Bureau, ask your local bank loan officer, or ask an accountant for references.

Spousal support. This differs greatly from state to state and judge to judge. Texas barely has any at all. To find out about how your local court is likely to deal with spousal support, see section F below, *How to learn about the law in your state.*

Child support. Child support takes priority. Only after the needs of children are satisfied will courts consider an award of spousal support. Then the court will try to balance the needs of one spouse against the ability to pay of the other.

Child support orders are always subject to modification, which means either parent can go back to court at any time to seek a change. To get a modification, it is generally necessary to show that needs or circumstances have changed since the last order. Spousal support orders might or might not be modifiable, depending on the wording in your agreement.

Child support and the mandatory guidelines

How much? You don't have to spend another minute wondering or arguing about this question as the matter has already been settled by guidelines in every state.

Mandatory child support guidelines. Every state now has child support guidelines that define the amount any judge in the state must award if the matter has to be decided in court. Subject to the judge's approval, parents can agree to any *reasonable* amount in a written settlement agreement, but if the matter of child support ends up in court, it will be decided according the child support guidelines for your state based on financial data proved to the judge by admissible financial documents or other evidence.

Additional support. In addition to guideline support, parents must arrange for health care for the child if it is available through the employment of either parent, and parents must share health care costs not covered by insurance equally (50/50) unless agreed otherwise by the parents.

Demonstrated financial data. Guidelines are based on income of the parents and, in some states, certain expenses that can be deducted. A judge can only consider financial data that can be

Child support takes priority. Only after the needs of children are satisfied will courts consider an award of spousal support.

demonstrated by admissible documents like pay stubs and financial statements, so you can't expect one parent to agree to financial claims of the other parent that can't be supported by documents.

If you show each other your financial records and apply the data to the guideline, there's really nothing left to argue about. Why waste the money it costs to go to court if you already know what the judge will order?

Exception—imputed income. If it can be shown in court that a parent is capable of earning more at a full-time job when such jobs are available, but chooses to work less or work at a lower-paying job, a judge could decide to set child support based on the amount the parent could be earning rather than actual income. For example, if a qualified mechanic lives where such jobs are available but chooses to make a bare living as a free-lance writer, that parent should not be surprised if a judge figures support based on what a mechanic earns. In other words, you have to do your best for your child(ren).

Only use information from your state's official site.

Get the official guidelines for your state

I keep a table of links to official child support information for every state on the CD and at **www.nolodivorce.com/CS**. Go there as soon as possible and get the child support guidelines for your state. Share the guideline information with the other parent and show each other your financial records. You'd have to do this in court anyway, so you might as well do it voluntarily without going to court. Apply the guidelines to data that can be documented and you've got the amount of support a judge would award. What's there to argue about?

Use only official information. You can't be sure that information found on a private web site is current, complete or accurate. Every state has an official site with a lot of information, worksheets, and calculators. Only use information from your state's official site.

Do not use online calculators on private sites because you can't be sure they are accurate. The ones we've seen have been incomplete and lack adequate instructions and guidance. For example, they might tell you to enter the "net income" for each parent without telling you how "net income" is defined in your state. Many states have a complex set of definitions for that figure. Many calculators do not include various deductions or exceptions that the state guidelines include.

CALIFORNIA IS A SPECIAL CASE

California guidelines are so incredibly complicated that lawyers and judges use a computer program that costs about $500 to figure the correct guideline amount and lawyers charge a stiff fee each time they run the program for you. Most people want several runs, based on a variety of "what if" possibilities or changes in income or deductions. The results of a program cannot be used in court unless it has been certified accurate by the California Judicial Council, so don't bother using online programs or any service that has not been certified.

Do not use online calculators on private sites because you can't be sure they are accurate.

To help you get what you need, I created **CalSupport,** a very affordable professional-quality program that has been certified by the Judicial Council every year since 1995, yet it costs only $34.95. **CalSupport** is just as powerful as professional software, only it is better: easier to use and easier to understand. For more about how to get the correct amount for guideline child support in California or for a trial version of CalSupport, go to **www.nolodivorce.com/CA**.

Who can help?

Every state has an office that helps establish and collect child support. If you have questions or want help with child support, this is the first place to call. If they are very busy, it might take some time to get assistance, but call and find out what they do and how they can help you. A table of links to official child support enforcement agencies for each state is on my web site at **www. nolodivorce.com/CS** and on the CD. Some states have more than one agency that can help establish or enforce a child support order, so also call your county court clerk's office and ask them for the name of the local office that helps people with child support issues.

F. How to learn about the law in your state

You will want to know more about the laws of your state and how they apply to the facts of your case. You especially want to know how clearly it can be predicted what a judge would do if presented with the facts of your case.

In some states, like California, the laws are so detailed and clear that the outcome—what any judge would do if given your facts—is quite predictable in most situations. This is a great help in negotiation, because the spouses can simply refer to the laws and use them as a guide in settling differences.

In other states, the laws can be so vague, or the judges are given so much discretion, that the only predictable thing is that no one can guess the outcome and you will have to spend a great deal on lawyers and legal proceedings to find out what some judge will order. In such states, it is even more important to settle your issues yourselves or in mediation, because you do not want to leave your life and your future to some stranger who doesn't know anything about you.

You especially want to know how clearly it can be predicted what a judge would do if presented with the facts of your case.

In addition to the law, you also want to know practical things, like where papers are filed, how long it takes to get a judgment, and what the filing fee is for filing a divorce. Here are some ways you can get information about the laws of your state.

Books. The cheapest way would be to read a self-help book on divorce laws of your state. Nolo Press Occidental publishes the famous *How to Do Your Own Divorce* books in California and Texas. For other states, go to a book store or library and search the Books In Print subject matter catalog under "Divorce," where you will find a section of state-by-state listings. Many states have self-help divorce books, but the quality ranges from excellent to terrible and it may not be easy to tell the difference. Do not use a book that says it's good in all 50 states as it is simply not true and probably is not good in your state. The worst thing would be an old book that has not kept up with changes, leaving you to read about laws that no longer exist and working with wrong information, so check the date of printing. Ask a reference librarian to make recommendations.

Do not use a book that says it's good in all 50 states as it is simply not true and probably is not good in your state.

Ask an attorney. This is the easiest, quickest and most reliable way, but not the cheapest. Still, good advice is worth a lot. I strongly recommend asking a family law attorney who limits his/her practice to mediation. This way you are more likely to get balanced advice aimed at solving problems and working your case toward settlement.

In California, call **Divorce Helpline,** a different kind of law firm that exists only to help people get through divorce. Their attorneys are expert at helping people solve problems and reach settlement. Working in offices across the state or everywhere by mail, phone, and fax, they offer legal information, advice, help with negotiations and mediation. They draft settlement agreements and do your paperwork for you, all at fixed fees for services. They will work with both spouses if you want them to. If you have a California case, call **(800) 359-7004** or go online to **www.divorcehelp.com**. It's the best thing in divorce services.

You can go see a family law attorney, but first read about choosing and using a lawyer in chapter 7, *I want someone to help me—Who can I call?* Getting information from a lawyer can be relatively reasonable and efficient if you go prepared and have specific goals in mind. Learn as much as you can ahead of time. It is best to find a lawyer who specializes in divorce—at least 50% of their case load.

I strongly recommend that you get advice from a lawyer trained in divorce mediation for whom mediation is at least 50% of his/her practice. Mediation-minded attorneys are more likely to give you neutral and problem-solving advice, whereas traditional attorneys tend to be more oriented to conflict and their advice tends to be adversarial.

Getting information from a lawyer can be relatively reasonable and efficient if you go prepared and have specific goals in mind.

Make sure the attorney understands that you are there only for information and advice and that you are not, at this time, retaining them to handle your case. In fact, it will be best if you never retain an attorney at all, as you will discover in the next chapter.

Before your first visit to an attorney, get yourself prepared by working through to chapter 6, step 7. The more informed and clear you are, the faster and cheaper you can get what you need. If you don't know what you want to find out, or if you can't make up your mind about things, wait until your mind clears. Otherwise you can end up paying $150-350 an hour for hand-holding, or you might get talked into legal action you don't need.

G. Tax issues

There can be important tax consequences to any divorce decision that involves money or property. Pay special attention to:

- Your tax filing status
- How to file returns during the separation period
- Dividing major items of marital property
- Capital gains tax liability, tax basis, and "rollovers"
- Designating support as child support or "family support"

Spouses who cooperate are in a better position to save money on taxes so you should try to work things out cooperatively for tax savings, if for no other reason.

Spouses who cooperate are in a better position to save money on taxes so you should try to work things out cooperatively for tax savings, if for no other reason.

Filing status. Your marital status on December 31 determines how you can file your tax returns:

- If legally married on December 31, you can file as Married Filing Joint or Married Filing Separately, an unfavorable status that is used if you can't get information from your spouse or don't want to share tax liability. You can also file as Head of Household if you have been separated for the last six months of the year and maintain a household for a qualified dependent.

- If divorced or separated by court order by December 31, you can file as Single, not a favorable status, or you can use the more favorable Head of Household status if you maintain a home for a qualified dependent. This may influence the terms of your parenting arrangement to enable a high-earner to use Head of Household so the parents can share the tax savings.

- You can share the child deduction by doing tax returns for both parents to find out how much is saved in taxes by reassigning child deductions and the parent who saves the most takes the deduction and pays the other parent the amount of increased taxes incurred by releasing the child deductions. This way both parents win and only the government loses.

Dividing major items of property can easily have important tax consequences. This is discussed briefly on page 56 in this chapter. Get advice before dividing a house or any other major capital item.

Child support and family support. Child support is not included in the income of the recipient and cannot be deducted from the income of the payor. Spousal support is included in the income of the recipient and deducted from the income of the payor. You can agree to pay all or part of child support as "family support" which is treated like spousal support. This means the high earner can save on taxes by deducting the payments from income, and the savings can be shared by the couple. Get advice before drafting such an agreement because it won't work if it is not worded exactly right.

Your local IRS office has very useful free booklets. Be sure to get publication 504, *Divorced or Separated Individuals,* which is full of valuable information. Also consider publications 523, *Selling Your Home,* and 503, *Child and Dependent Care Expenses.* Depending on how much money and property you have, you might find it worth the cost to consult a tax expert before making decisions and especially before entering into a settlement agreement.

Dividing major items of property can easily have important tax consequences.

5

STRATEGIES FOR THE DIFFICULT DIVORCE

STRATEGY MEANS HAVING A PLAN, in this case your plan for how to get what you want and what's fair in your legal divorce—division of marital property, support, and parenting arrangements. The first step in your plan is to decide whether you are better off starting (or continuing) legal actions in court or taking a more moderate approach by doing things that will help move your case toward negotiation and mediation. War or peace? Hardball or soft? After discussing this in sections A–D, I'll explain in sections E and F the best ways to prepare and start your case (if it hasn't already started).

Never start litigation or threaten it unless you have no better alternative.

A. The general rule

For most people in most cases, the best strategy is to read this book clear through chapter 6 to learn all of the steps you can take to reduce conflict, increase confidence and trust on both sides so you can settle the terms of your divorce through negotiation or mediation or by using collaborative lawyers, none of which involve fighting in court. **Never start litigation** (court action) or threaten it unless you have no better alternative, and even then you should stay alert for opportunities to move your case out of court and toward negotiation, mediation, or collaborative lawyers—discussed in section E below—none of which involve fighting in court.

B. When litigation makes sense

Litigation means the actions you or a lawyer can take in court that are illustrated on page 17. So, your real question is whether there is something you need that you can't do without and can't get some other way, but you believe you can get it from:

- **Pretrial motions** asking for orders for temporary support, custody and visitation, and if needed, restraining orders protecting people and/or property.

- **Formal discovery** where you demand answers under oath to get information from your Ex that you need but can't get any by any of the self-help methods discussed in the Appendix.

- **Trial,** where some stranger (the judge) hears a brief and limited version of your story, then imposes decisions on you about your property, child and/or spousal support, parenting schedules, and restraining orders for keeping the peace in high-conflict cases.

You should always be prepared to fend for yourself in practical ways, wherever and however you can.

The problem, of course, is that it costs a lot to hire an attorney to do discovery or get orders for you. What's worse, people who have had orders shoved down their throats don't necessarily do what they've been told. Then you're left with the practical problem of enforcing your orders, and that means more trips to court for more orders, more trips for threats of fines or jail for contempt of court and eventually, after many trips to court, the offender might spend a few days in jail, for all the good that might do you. Some people are more likely than others to be impressed by court orders, but it's not exactly an ideal solution. Even so, these legal remedies might be better than nothing and they're all the law has to offer. You should always be prepared to fend for yourself in practical ways, wherever and however you can.

With that said, let's look at situations where legal action makes sense.

1. **Fear for the safety of yourself or your child.** If your spouse is an habitual controller/abuser—that is, has abused several times in the past—and you fear it will happen again soon, read chapter 1D, *Domestic Abuse and Violence.* You need to find a safe place to go, you need to work with a DV counselor and get into a DV support group. At some point, you might decide to go to court for restraining orders along with orders for spousal and/or child support, child custody and property possession and protection orders. Go get help.

2. **Desperately broke.** If your finances are truly desperate and frightening—*or if your spouse feels this way*—read chapter 6, step 4, then consider your options. You should do whatever you can to take care of yourself for a few weeks or a few months while you read this material and try to make temporary arrangements with your spouse for financial support. Going to court for support orders is a reasonable option, but the attorney will be expensive and only a few will start without being paid before taking your case. Where will you get the fee?

3. **Divorce papers served on you.** If you've been served with papers by your Ex and it's nothing more than a petition or complaint starting a divorce, that's not so bad. If you want to participate in court and have some say in the outcome, you need to file a response before the deadline stated on your papers. If it has passed, call the court clerk and ask if you are still able to file a response even though the deadline has passed. If so, quickly file a response. If not, you'll need an attorney to help you make a motion to allow you to enter the case late (read chapter 7). Another option is to get a letter from whoever filed the papers (your ex or ex's lawyer) stating in writing that he/she will not move forward without

At some point, you might decide to go to court for restraining orders along with orders for spousal and/ or child support, child custody and property possession and protection orders.

30 days' written notice and an opportunity to file a response at that time.

If a hearing has been scheduled to determine support or child custody issues, you need to get an attorney right away to represent you at the hearing or seek a continuance so you can prepare. Read chapter 7 about what kind of attorney to get. If you don't have time to get an attorney, show up at the time and place indicated on your papers and ask the judge for a continuance to allow you time to get an attorney to represent you. Meanwhile, if you're on speaking terms with your spouse, ask why things started off this way. A lot of attorneys do it routinely, whether the case needs it or not, thinking it "good" practice. If that's the case, maybe you can get your spouse to get the attorney to withdraw the motions while you two go into mediation to work out some temporary terms. But do not fail to show up at the hearing, no matter what your spouse says. Or, you could call the court clerk the morning of or day before and ask if your case has been taken off the calendar.

If a hearing has been scheduled to determine support or child custody issues, you need to get an attorney right away.

4. **Fear of sneak attack**. If you are afraid your spouse might do something bad once he/she finds out you want a divorce or are starting one, you can take steps to defend yourself or you can go on the offense and strike first. This is such an ambiguous and dangerous situation that I am going to discuss it separately in section D below.

5. **Bullies and stubborn resisters**. If your spouse is a bully, a controller, and you've tried everything else, you might have to take action in court to show that you won't be intimidated and are serious about moving forward. If your spouse is not a controller but is sullenly dragging things out and frustrating every effort to move toward a settlement, read the sidebar article in chapter 6, step 8, about how to deal with passive resistance.

6. **Upset, anger, fear of doing it alone.** If you want a lawyer to "get" your spouse or prove your independence, you will definitely end up hurting yourself badly no matter what happens to your spouse, not to mention your children if you have any. Don't do it. If you feel you can't get through this alone, look for a collaborative lawyer or a family lawyer-mediator to help you, but without litigation. Read chapter 5E and 7, *I want someone to help me—Who can I call?*

No matter what you do, no matter what happens, once the smoke clears and things settle down, finish this book and start working on ways to move your case away from litigation and toward negotiation or mediation.

C. The huge cost of legal battle

We can't talk about legal battle (litigation) without discussing the cost, and I bet you already know what I'm going to say—that's right, it's *scary huge!* More often than not, a legal battle is financially ruinous and emotionally devastating. True, there are situations where legal battle can't be avoided but there are compelling reasons why you should never go into litigation without exhausting every other option and once you are in litigation you should never stop looking for ways to limit the action or settle or move your case toward negotiation and mediation.

More often than not, a legal battle is financially ruinous and emotionally devastating.

When people ask me, "How much does a divorce cost?" I always ask, "How much do you have?" because unless you are very wealthy, a legal battle will consume everything and probably more. A word of warning: when an attorney says his/her retainer for a divorce is $2,500 or some other number, this does not mean that this is the total cost—it's just the beginning! Ask the attorney about final and total cost and you'll learn that there is no limit on how much you might end up paying.

So, what's average? Keeping in mind that costs vary greatly from state to state and from urban to rural areas and that no one has done a survey, an educated guess would be a range from a minimum of $12,000 up to $200,000 or more on each side! Even higher fees are not uncommon, while $25,000 each would be fortunate. This is money your family could put to better use, so you see that in terms of dollars, your family stands to lose a great deal in a legal battle.

Besides being financially ruinous, a contested divorce can wreck your own life for years to come, perhaps forever. If you have children, a legal battle can put them through a hell that can damage them forever. You can't put a price on the intense emotional stress that you and your kids will suffer for the months running into years that you spend battling, or the time it might take to recover, if ever you can.

If you have children, a legal battle can put them through a hell that can damage them forever.

Not only is legal battle expensive, but seeking solutions in court is notoriously ineffective. There are far better (and less expensive) ways to settle your issues, as you will learn in this book. Unless, that is, you have one of those rare cases discussed in the section above where some litigation is a good option.

D. Offense or defense? Fear of a sneak attack

This situation gets separate treatment because it is so ambiguous yet so dangerous if you guess wrong in either direction. This is why I wanted to discuss it after you got a sense of the financial and emotional cost involved in legal battle.

A worst-case scenario is spelled out in *Winning the Divorce War* by Ronald Sharp, a Michigan attorney. Most attorneys speak guardedly about the realities of their work in the legal system, but Sharp states bluntly that he works in an adversarial system where divorce is a war and the person you once loved is now your enemy, so start acting like it. And just look at the terrible consequence of his attitude! He opens with a chapter on "The Preemptive Strike," where he tells of a woman with no idea there was going to be a divorce who came home from work one day to find the house cleaned out, the children gone with their father to parts unknown, all accounts emptied, all credit cards canceled, and a man at the door handing her divorce papers. She asks the author how he can help her and he makes this revealing comment: "It would not be easy. Nor cheap. *Her husband must have read my book.*" The man did what this author recommends! Go for the throat! Declare war!

Well, yes, what happened to the woman is not unheard of, but it is quite rare. At no point does the author speak frankly about the terrible financial and emotional cost to the man himself or to his children or of the future parenting struggles, all because of the war the man started. The author doesn't say what the outcome was after the family was bankrupted by attorney fees, but in almost every case I know of, the couple eventually ends up with relatively typical orders, except the family is broke and trust is so shattered that the outlook for parenting children is bleak. Remember, children are most harmed by the parents' continued inability to resolve conflict and in this case, that won't come easily or soon.

Remember, children are most harmed by the parents' continued inability to resolve conflict.

A better result in the same case could have been obtained at much less emotional and financial cost and the future parenting might have been salvaged. If only the man had read my book!

Automatic restraining orders. Another thing Sharp left out is that many states have automatic restraining orders that are issued with every petition or complaint for divorce. Typically, both parties are ordered (1) not to remove a child from the state without prior written permission of the other parent or order of the court; (2) not to transfer, sell or borrow against *any* property except in the usual course of business or for necessities; (3) not to cancel, transfer or borrow against insurance held for the benefit of the other spouse or a minor child; (4) to notify the other party at least five days in advance of extraordinary expenses. In such states, the man in Sharp's sad story would have been in contempt of court at the outset and subject to penalties.

Defense. So now you come to this same question in your own case. Do you feel you need some defensive orders before you start working on a peaceful resolution? First, find out if your state issues automatic orders at the outset of every divorce (see chapter 4F, *How to learn about the law in your state*). If so, all you have to do is file for a divorce and you've got basic protections. If not, and if you think your spouse might act badly when the divorce is announced, you need an attorney to file your divorce with a motion for orders similar to the automatic ones mentioned above, or stronger ones if your spouse is an habitual abuser or controller.

You know your spouse better than anyone, so ultimately you are the only one who can decide how far you have to go to protect yourself and whether it is really necessary for you to strike the first blow and draw the first blood.

Offense. Some attorneys, like Mr. Sharp, would advise you to regard your spouse as an enemy and strike first by taking all money out of accounts, closing credit cards, and moving away with the kids. If your spouse is an habitual abuser/controller this might make sense, otherwise it's very poor advice indeed. If your spouse is by nature a bully who needs to be hit hard to see that you are determined and won't be intimidated, maybe *some* aggression is in order, but it would be a shame to create an enemy (or a worse enemy) where none yet exists or to miss a chance to keep a potential enemy from becoming one, especially if this person is also your child's parent or parent-figure.

Only you can decide. You know your spouse better than anyone, so ultimately you are the only one who can decide how far you have to go to protect yourself and whether it is really necessary for you to strike the first blow and draw the first blood. Please don't strike out of anger or a thirst for revenge, because in divorce you always end up hurting yourself as much as your spouse. If you want to take legal action because you fear what your spouse might do, you might remember that most fears never come true and if you harbor any uncertainty about your decision, talk to a counselor or a family law attorney who does both mediation and litigation to see if they think your concerns and planned actions are valid.

E. Better alternatives to legal action

There are two very good alternatives to the painful process of trying to solve divorce problems in court: mediation, or both parties being represented by collaborative lawyers.

Mediation

In mediation a couple is guided by a neutral professional who is trained and experienced at helping the parties communicate, learn about relevant laws, explore all available options for property, children and support, and discuss those options in a calm, safe, and constructive manner until they arrive at an agreement that seems fair and acceptable to both. This is much less stressful than a legal battle where tempers, stress, fear, cost and upset run high. The effect of working with a good mediator is almost magical.

The person who is better prepared and organized will generally do better in negotiation, mediation or court.

Mediation is not just for friendly divorces. Angry, conflicted couples are especially in need of mediation and stand to gain the most, especially if they have children.

The advantages of mediation are safety, privacy, speed, certainty, much less cost, much less stress, and better compliance with terms of judgment.
  • **Effective.** Mediation is effective at least 80% of the time, even in cases with high conflict, and most cases get settled in relatively few sessions. Some couples get results in one meeting, some might need ten meetings, but in every case it is far less expensive and takes less time than going to court.
  • **Private.** When you take your case to court everything about your marriage and personal affairs becomes a matter of public record, but mediation is confidential and private. Privacy is one of the big benefits of mediation.
  • **Cost.** For most couples, mediation will cost about 10% of what they would spend if they retain attorneys and go to court.

You need to be sure that your goals are realistic, given your facts, so this comes after you gather facts and it might mean learning about the laws of your state (chapter 4F) or perhaps getting advice from a family law attorney (chapter 7) who will know if your goals are reasonable given their experience with what judges in your area might order. Be sure to choose a family law attorney who is primarily a mediator rather than one who does litigation. Too many attorneys give advice that leads to litigation because that's what they do and that's how they earn the most.

The list of goals and the plans you make will stand behind every step you take and how you direct your attorney (if you get one); for example, initial motions or letters proposing terms, and so on. Your plan will be the common thread that pulls everything together and keeps you on track. You won't be blown off course by whatever your spouse does; instead, you will stick to your plan.

Understanding your spouse's emotional makeup can pay off in a big way.

Short and long-term plans

Your long-term plan is important, but you also need a short-term plan to cover the immediate future and the time while the divorce is pending (chapter 6, step 1). The short-term plan should be consistent with where you want to end up in the long term. For example, let's say your long-term goal is to encourage contact and bonding between the children and their other parent, and your parents are willing to watch the kids for free while you work your part-time job, but they are very antagonistic toward the other parent and say unpleasant things in front of the kids. This is a clear conflict between short-term convenience and long-term goal. You have to figure out which is more important in any situation where the short-term plan and long-term goals are in conflict.

Plans based on who you are dealing with

The emotional dynamic underlying your relationship is usually the key. This is not about the reasons you are getting divorced but the way in which you, your spouse, and attorneys (if any) approach problems. It is always the emotions, personalities, and attitudes of the players that drive the divorce process. Calm, reasonable people can divide up millions in a fairly short time, while an angry spouse can make the divorce drag on for years and consume marital assets along the way.

This means that when you deal with your spouse directly, it is more important than at any time in your life that you pay attention to the kind of person your spouse is—what makes him/her tick. Try to see your spouse objectively, not idealized as when you were in love and not demonized as you might feel right now. Be aware of strengths, weaknesses, patterns of behavior. Even more important is the matter of your own feelings and attitudes. If you can't keep business and personal stuff separate (chapter 6, step 6), you're going to need help negotiating, maybe a mediator, and you'll want to get advice to see if your plan is reasonable (see chapter 7).

It is difficult to settle with a spouse who is operating on wrong information or bad advice.

You know what kind of person your spouse is, so don't fight it, use it! Put that knowledge to work, let it be your guide for how you deal with your spouse. When the deal's done, you can do whatever you want, but for now don't let your emotions get in the way of business. Review chapters 3 and 6 for ideas about how to deal with your spouse and with yourself. Understanding your spouse's emotional makeup can pay off in a big way. Understanding yourself and breaking bad habits can pay off even more. Here are some examples of how the relationship between personalities can affect the way you conduct your case:

Insecure, upset spouses. Divorce tends to undermine self-confidence for most people and in most relationships one spouse feels at a disadvantage because the other has handled business and financial affairs and has more knowledge and experience with such things. It will help *you* if you help your spouse gain confidence and trust around the negotiations. I discussed what both of you can do to improve this situation in chapter 3F, so please review that now.

Very insecure people might feel a lot better being represented by an attorney, so in that case your goal is to get your spouse to use a collaborative lawyer (chapters 5E and 7) who will represent him/her and conduct negotiation or mediation without going to court. If you can afford it, offer to cover some or all of the cost of doing it this way.

Unreal expectations, wrong ideas. People get unreal expectations from a lot of places: TV, friends, relatives or the hairdresser. Wherever it comes from, it is difficult to settle with a spouse who is operating on wrong information or bad advice. The cure for this is to make sure he/she gets reliable information in a form that he/she can accept. Start by giving him/her this book, then discuss the parts that apply to your case. If you can afford it, pay for your spouse to get advice from a divorce specialist attorney-mediator. You might discuss getting a mediator to help you settle issues you don't agree on.

You need to plan carefully when and how you deliver the message that you want a divorce because the way you do this will set the tone for the future.

Spouses in denial, resisting. Sometimes a spouse does not want a divorce. You don't need cooperation to get a divorce and no legal action can force you to stay married, but some spouses resist and obstruct any way they can. A spouse in only mild denial will come out of it when they get the first divorce papers and see that it is really going to happen. Some who are not in touch with their own feelings do not realize why they fight each step along the way. Read the sidebar article about passive resistance at chapter 6, step 8.

Controllers. If your spouse has a controlling personality, you need to understand that having control is a deep-seated need and that not being in control creates huge fears, so they fight for control passionately and beyond all reason, as if they were fighting for their lives—and much about divorce makes them feel out of control. Normal people hate the legal process and want to get out of it as soon as possible. Controlling people will see it as a new arena in which they need control.

Especially if you hope for cooperative parenting in the future, you might take some time to let your spouse regain balance. Let your spouse feel he/she does have some control and can call many of the shots so long as the divorce moves forward eventually and the result is fair to both of you. Explain that litigation means less control by far, because in working out an agreement they get to say what they'll accept and what they won't, whereas in court the lawyers call the shots and some stranger (the judge) who does not know or care about your family will impose a decision, like it or not. Let your spouse make decisions that really aren't important to you, like when you meet, how to conduct negotiations, and so on.

If you aren't making headway on your own, try to get your spouse to agree to mediation where you'd be better off with an experienced mediator who comes from a family counseling background.

One of your main goals in the divorce process is to break free from your spouse's control, but this might be best done after the divorce rather than at the outset. If you can postpone your own need to be free, you can take some time and effort to go along with your spouse and help him/her continue to feel some control.

If all else fails, you'll want to hire a family law attorney-mediator who also does some litigation, or a hard-core litigator if you expect a fierce battle. Read the rest of this book and stay alert for opportunities to move your case toward negotiation or mediation. Read chapter 9, *How to win a legal battle.*

Things will go a lot more smoothly if you can wait for your spouse to accept the idea of the divorce and agree to it before you start your case.

G. The best way to start a divorce

You need to plan carefully when and how you deliver the message that you want a divorce because the way you do this will set the tone for the future. If you are dealing with an abuser/controller, there's not much point in talking until you establish a position of power. If you are planning a surprise attack for any reason, you would not tip your hand. But, **in all other cases** it is very important to take some time to prepare your spouse and let him/her get used to the idea that a divorce is going to happen.

Typically, one spouse is ready to act long before the other has accepted the idea of a divorce and this is a common cause of conflict. Things will go a lot more smoothly if you can wait for your spouse to accept the idea of the divorce and agree to it before you start your case. Ideally, you will not file for a divorce before you've had a chance to use the concepts in chapters 3 and 6 to help reduce conflict, solve problems and move your case toward negotiation, mediation or collaborative law, none of which involve a battle in court. However, there are situations where you need to get a divorce on file for strategic reasons or because you need to be single by December 31 so you can file your tax return as a single person.

It is very important to prepare your spouse so he/she doesn't get upset and rush off and hire an attorney who will probably take your case into litigation.

Softening the blow

No matter when you file for your divorce, whether your spouse has accepted the idea or not, it is **very important** to prepare your spouse ahead of time, soften the blow, and file your papers in such a way that your spouse is under no immediate pressure to file a response, no need to run to an attorney because there's plenty of time to work on a settlement.

Put yourself in your spouse's position and imagine what is feels like to suddenly be handed threatening legal documents. For example, this is what people in California see on their Summons:

> You have 30 calendar days after this Summons and Petition are served on you to file a Response at the court and have a copy served on the petitioner. A letter or phone call will not protect you. If you do not file your Response on time, the court may make orders affecting your marriage or domestic partnership, your property, and custody of your children. You may be ordered to pay support and

attorney fees and costs. If you want legal advice, contact a lawyer immediately.

In Texas, the recipient sees this on the Citation:

> Notice to Defendant: You have been sued. You may employ an attorney. If you or your attorney do not file a written answer with the clerk who issued this citation by 10:00 a.m. on the Monday next following the expiration of twenty days after you were served this citation and petition, a default judgment may be taken against you.

These are representative of all states. Getting legal documents that appear so urgent and threatening is shocking and likely to create either anger or fear or both unless the recipient is properly prepared—something very few attorneys ever think to do. It is very important to prepare your spouse so he/she doesn't get upset and rush off and hire an attorney who will probably take your case into litigation.

In addition to advance notice and discussion, tell your spouse that you have created a period of safety so he/she will be under no pressure to respond and that the notice to reply within so many days can be ignored. Say that you are doing this so there will be plenty of time for you to work out the terms of your settlement. There are two ways to do this and you can use one, the other, or both.

- The greatest sense of security can be created if, rather than listing your marital and separate property, you state in your petition that property will be divided in a settlement agreement. Some states include this option in their forms; in other states you type in "To be determined by written agreement" in the place where marital or separate property are to be described. This means that if you do not reach an agreement, you have to file an amended

Good

information

really helps.

petition that lists all property that is involved in your case and therefore no response is required until that happens.

- Another way would be to list marital and separate property in your petition and send a formal letter signed by you (or your attorney if you have one) promising that no further legal steps will be taken and the case will not be moved forward unless you first give the respondent 30 days' written notice that you intend to do so.

If you have an attorney, you have to instruct him/her to do things this way because they rarely think of it themselves.

Give your spouse a copy of this book and discuss this section. Good information really helps.

6

TEN STEPS TO A BETTER DIVORCE

THESE STEPS WILL HELP YOU reduce conflict, stress, pain and avoid the huge expense of a court battle. The profiles in chapter 1 will help you focus on which of these steps are most important to you, though it can't hurt to browse through them all.

Each step is a foundation for steps that follow.

Remember the general rules from the beginning of this book:

> **General rule 1.** Unless you have an emergency, do not talk to an attorney (or continue, if you've started) until you read through Step 7.

> **General rule 2.** Try to avoid talking to your spouse about your divorce until you've read through Step 8.

> **General rule 3.** Any time you feel you want to get personal assistance rather than continue here, read chapter 7, *I want someone to help me—Who can I call?*

Each step is a foundation for steps that follow. That is, unless you satisfy an earlier step, it might be more difficult to succeed in steps that follow.

Step 1. Short-term safety and stability

If physical safety for you or your children is a concern, read chapter 1D.

Start with short-term solutions. Your first step is to do whatever it takes to arrange short-term safety, stability, and security for yourself, your children, and your spouse—in that order. Not forever—just for a month or a few months at a time—and I'm talking about minimum living conditions, not your old standard of living, not yet, just whatever it takes to get some breathing room. Other than reading this book and thinking about things, try not to do much else until you plan arrangements for how you'll get by for a short time.

Do whatever it takes to arrange short-term safety, stability, and security for yourself, your children, and your spouse—in that order.

Help yourself if you can. If necessary get a job. Call on friends or relatives for help, perhaps a place to stay. If you are in a faith community, go there. Public assistance is a last resort because it can get you tangled in bureaucratic frustrations that you would rather not have to deal with now, but it is there if nothing else is possible.

You can't think straight or make sound decisions if you don't know where you will live or how you will eat, or if you are afraid for your safety or if you think your house might be foreclosed or your car repossessed. You can't negotiate a settlement if your spouse is not also in a safe and stable situation and able to think calmly.

You want to avoid the fear that drives people into attorney's offices. If you can't get both spouses stabilized, the fear and upset level will go up until one of you goes to an attorney for help and then you will probably end up in court with attorneys arguing pretrial motions—dragged into the legal system at the beginning. Legal procedures are tremendously upsetting and very expensive, on the order of tens of thousands of dollars—*at least!* You *really* would like to avoid this, if possible.

You need some time to step back, get calm, let things quiet down while you take the next steps, get information, get organized, think things out calmly, get reliable advice, decide what to do next. You want to work on reducing emotional upset—at least your own—and this takes some time. You'd like to work on mutual acceptance of the divorce, and this takes time.

If you're okay, at least for a while, do what you can to help your spouse feel stable and secure about money, at least in the short-term, and contact with the kids. You don't want him/her running in fear for an attorney and you can't negotiate or co-parent with a spouse who does not know how the bills will get paid or when he/she will see the children next. A little reassurance can go a long way here.

Reduce stress and conflict. Both of you should read chapter 3F and work on reducing stress and conflict, not just between you but within yourselves.

Be very careful where you get advice. Your friends and relatives will be a fountain of free advice, *but don't take it*—the price is too high if they're wrong. They mean well, but probably don't know what they're talking about. You *should* use your friends for emotional support, but take advice only from an attorney who specializes in divorce. Don't take advice from paralegals or people who run typing services; they're not trained for it. In California, you can call Divorce Helpline at (800) 359-7004 and consult their attorneys.

Step 2. Protect children

Every time you get on an airplane, a flight attendant explains that if the oxygen masks come down, put *yours* on first, *before* you help children. This is because if you pass out, you won't be able to help them. It's the same here: if you're not okay, your children can't be okay. They are exceedingly sensitive to your mood. Look at it

You need some time to step back, get calm, let things quiet down.

from your child's point of view. They are totally dependent on both parents for their sense of safety and well-being. They absorb from you what life is like and how people live. Think how upsetting it is when the two people they depend on are in constant tension and unhappy most of the time, when the only home they know is frequently unpleasant to live in because of stress and conflict.

Review the last pages of chapter 3, *Getting children through a tough time.*

Children need their relationship with both parents.

Children need their relationship with both parents. There is bonding that cannot easily be replaced by a surrogate parent or stepparent. To protect the essential parent-child relationship, you have to insulate children from your own conflict with their other parent. The divorce is not their problem; it's yours. Being a bad wife or husband doesn't make your spouse a bad parent, so don't hold the children hostage—they are not pawns or bartering pieces in your struggle. In the area of custody and visitation, don't bargain with your spouse on any other basis than what will give your children the most stability and the best contact with both parents.

Bad mom, bad dad. Short of abuse, which is discussed in chapter 1D, if you feel the other parent is bad for the children and you want to limit contact with them or even have it supervised, you must first be certain your view isn't the result of your own upset. Visit a child psychologist or family therapist for an objective opinion (chapter 7E). The counselor might need to see the children, too. If the counselor agrees with you, ask your spouse to visit the counselor. Without an agreement between parents or convincing evidence, courts don't like to severely limit the other parent's access, so you might end up in a legal battle on this point. If so, try to agree to other issues and limit your disagreement to just this one thing. Try to get your spouse into mediation or representation by collaborative lawyers to help settle the matter (chapter 7), but also be prepared for a legal battle.

The worst thing for the child of a broken home is feeling responsible for the breakup and feeling that loving one parent is a betrayal of the other. These feelings cause children intense stress and insecurity. To protect your child from almost unbearable pain, don't say anything bad about the other parent in front of the child; don't undermine or interfere in any way with the child's relationship with or love for the other parent; don't put the child in a position of having to take sides. Do encourage every possible kind of constructive relationship your child can have with your ex-mate. Let the children know that you are happy when they have a good, loving time with their other parent.

Kids can really get on your nerves at a time like this and single parenting is enough to overwhelm any normal person. You are not Superman or She-Ra, the Princess of Power, and kids are not designed to be raised by one lone person. You need help and support, and you need time off from the kids. Maybe the other parent can take over for a few hours or days. Ask for help from family, friends and parent support groups and family service agencies in your area. Get references to groups in your area through temples, churches, social service agencies or yellow pages.

Let the children know that you are happy when they have a good, loving time with their other parent.

Studies show that harm to children is more closely related to conflict after the divorce. Everyone has conflict before and during a divorce, but if you want to protect your children, get finished with the conflict and resolve it, at least within yourself, as quickly as possible.

Step 3. Early practical steps

There are practical things you can do that will help your case, build your sense of confidence, save money and reduce your need for an attorney or court action. On the personal level, chapter 3 is about things you can do to reduce anger, insecurity and fear, while this chapter is devoted to steps you can take to reduce conflict, improve communication and move your case toward negotiation or mediation.

- If divorce has not been announced but you are sure one is coming, and if you are not planning a surprise attack (chapter 5), take time to work on mutual acceptance of the divorce and other elements of the good divorce (chapter 3A).

- Start building a nest egg to help you through the first few months.

- Build your own credit. If you don't have credit cards in your own name, apply for one or more right now. To establish good credit, use your cards instead of cash and be sure to always pay the bill by the due date.

If you need more income, think about ways you can earn it.

- If you have children, keep a log of time you spend with them and things you do for them and also track your spouse's child visits and chores. If your record is on the low side, increase your contact and contributions. You may never need this information, but it might be useful if there's a disagreement over the parenting schedule.

- As soon as you feel able, start using the worksheets on the CD to organize your personal and financial facts. Make photocopies of every family financial record you can find. In a nutshell, you need a list of all family assets and debts. For details on how to do this, see step 6 below and the Appendix.

- The Budget Worksheet is especially important as you need to know what you have been spending and estimate what it will cost both spouses to live separately. If you need more income, think about ways you can earn it.

Think about getting more education or training to prepare for a better job.

- **It is *very* important** at some early point to actually close all credit card accounts and accounts that were in use during your marriage—it is not enough to simply have your name removed. Open new accounts and get new credit cards in your separate names. Give written notice to all creditors that either party might have dealt with during the marriage—tell them that you are separated and will no longer be responsible for your partner's debts. Important! Unless you are planning a surprise attack (chapter 5) be sure to inform your spouse well in advance when you close accounts or take other steps that could have an effect on his/her life, otherwise it will cause trouble, seem like an attack and create unnecessary upset.

- **Withdraw funds?** If you are sure that your spouse is going to fight you over your share of family assets, consider withdrawing half of the money in joint accounts before you inform your spouse that you have done so. This will be correctly understood as a hostile act that will create upset and undermine trust, so only do it if you feel you have no better choice.

Step 4. Money and parenting in the early stages

Money

If your spouse depends on you to pay the bills and you don't give some reassurance that you'll help, your spouse will be forced to get an attorney and file for a support order—then your life gets dragged into court, lawyer wars, conflict and huge expense. Much better if you promise to help with the bills until you've both had some time to think, adjust, discuss the terms of your separation.

It is very important at some early point to actually close all credit card accounts and accounts that were in use during your marriage—it is not enough to simply have your name removed.

Be very reassuring. Ask your spouse to look at this book and work with you on these steps. Offer to make a temporary agreement in writing that will reassure both of you about money and parenting, just for the short term.

If you depend on your spouse to pay the bills, your goal is to get stable and secure for a few weeks or months while you figure out what to do next.

It will be better for both of you to make a temporary arrangement without having to drag your case into court.

- Send a polite message to your spouse, either in a letter or through a diplomatic friend or clergyman—someone who will definitely not add to the tension—that if you can't work out a temporary agreement to keep bills paid at least for a few months, you will have no choice but to get an attorney and go for a court order. You really don't want to do this because it will be hugely upsetting and expensive, an unnecessary waste that will be bad for everyone. Explain that it will be better for both of you to make a temporary arrangement without having to drag your case into court.

- Give your spouse a copy of this book and discuss this section.

- Think of ways you can take care of yourself, or maybe you can get help from friends or family or your faith community.

Child support. Read chapter 4E, then go to **www.nolodivorce. com/CS** for the link to official child support information and guidelines for your state.

If nothing works with your spouse and you can't get short-term help from friends or family, you have three choices:

1. If your spouse has wages or assets you can attach for support, you can get an attorney and go to court for a support order. Read chapter 7, *I want someone to help me—Who can I call?*

2. Every state has an office in charge of obtaining child support orders and enforcing them. Ask the clerk at the courthouse how to contact them.

3. If your spouse doesn't work or changes employers frequently or otherwise isn't worth taking to court for support, you'll have to try to get help from friends, relatives, your faith group or public assistance until you can support yourself on your own. Focus on stability first, then come back here and carry on with the rest of the steps.

Parenting

The parent with the children might fear that there won't be enough money to live on or that the other parent will take the kids and not return them.

The parent without the children might be afraid of not being able to see them frequently and regularly.

If you break up with no agreement or understanding for how children will be supported or when they will have contact with both parents, this can create anxiety that will drive a parent into a lawyer's office, thus dragging your family into court. It would be a lot better if you could avoid this.

For the good of your children, yourselves, and your futures, it is essential that you each reassure the other that your personal problems will not interfere with the children having regular contact

It is essential that you each reassure the other that your personal problems will not interfere with the children having regular contact with both parents and that they will have enough support to live on.

with both parents and that they will have enough support to live on, as close as possible to the way they lived before your breakup.

You can both calm your concerns by making a temporary agreement with a schedule for when each parent will have the care of the children and how they will be supported. The agreement should be in writing and can be described as temporary for a certain number of months or until you make a full and final settlement.

Step 5. Temporary agreements

During the early days of your separation, if you two can work out your own temporary arrangements for paying the bills and parenting the children, neither of you will need an attorney to go to court for temporary orders.

If you two can work out your own temporary arrangements for paying the bills and parenting the children, neither of you will need an attorney to go to court for temporary orders.

- Start by agreeing that you want a fair result and will both act fairly.

- Agree to communicate before doing anything that will affect the other or the estate or the children. The goal here is to avoid surprises and upset, including things like closing accounts or starting legal actions.

- Agree in writing that if you are not able to work things out between you, you will not go to court—instead, you will go to mediation and if that doesn't work you'll use arbitration.

You don't have to do everything at once, but rather you can start with things you can agree on, like those terms suggested above, then build as you go along. Put your temporary agreements in writing.

A sample agreement that you can use as a guide for language for your temporary agreement is on the CD in the back of this book. Just use parts that are about the temporary terms you can agree on. You can write your agreement neatly by hand or prepare it on a computer or typewriter, whatever you have available. Make one copy for each of you to hold. At the beginning, put "This agreement is binding for __ weeks/months" or (this is best) "until a permanent agreement is reached or, if we can't reach one, until judgment is imposed."

Your goal is to create enough financial and parenting reassurance that both parties can move further along in these steps and are able to work out the final terms for your divorce.

Step 6. Get organized and take care of business

The business end of divorce is about the decisions you need to make about property, debts, support and parenting if you have children. Because the choices and decisions you make now can influence your well-being for the rest of your days, getting your facts organized so you can make those decisions is very important.

Because the choices and decisions you make now can influence your well-being for the rest of your days, getting your facts organized so you can make those decisions is very important.

Generally speaking, the person who is better prepared will do better in negotiations, mediation or in court. Before you enter negotiation or mediation, you want to be prepared. It is common for one spouse to have more information and experience, therefore more negotiating power than the other and that makes for an imbalance of power and a more difficult negotiation. This problem can be improved if the less-confident spouse will get organized, informed and prepared. Even if you are in the middle of a divorce, it is not too late—just follow the instructions in this section and watch everything start to make sense and your self-confidence rise.

Be sure to read the closely related discussion in chapter 5E about planning.

Decisions are based on facts. To get a divorce, you have to make decisions about how to divide marital property and debts, how much spousal support will be paid (if any), and if you have children, how to arrange for their support and shared parenting. Making decisions—knowing what you want—is based on two things: the facts of your case and how the law affects those facts in your state.

Worksheets. I put a list of facts and documents you'll need in the Appendix, and to help you organize your information I put several worksheets on the CD that comes with this book. These are exactly the sort of worksheets any good attorney would use to organize your case, including:

Making decisions— knowing what you want—is based on two things: the facts of your case and how the law affects those facts in your state.

- Personal Information
- Assets and Debts
- Budget
- Parental Activities (who does what now and who'll do it after)

Read the Appendix and use these worksheets to get your facts and your thoughts in order. If you prepare your case with these worksheets and gather supporting documents before you visit an attorney (if you ever want to) you will save hours of attorney time and hundreds or thousands of dollars. You will impress the attorney as being someone who is prepared and knows what they are doing. Even if you never see an attorney, you will feel more in charge of things yourself.

The law. Deciding what you want requires an understanding of what you are entitled to under the laws of your state and whether those laws provide a clearly predictable outcome if your case were to end up in court. In some states, like California, the law is so detailed that on most matters you can predict what any judge would decide with a given set of facts. In other states, the decision is mostly in the discretion in the judge, so no one can say exactly what one judge or another might decide at any given time. In these states, your decisions must be based on your own sense of what seems reasonable and fair to both parties. Read chapter 4F, *How to learn about the law,* then if you want legal advice, read chapter 7, *I want someone to help me—Who can I call?*

More about decisions. Don't make long-term decisions when you are upset, because your judgment isn't sound and you don't want to build the rest of your life on decisions based on anger, guilt or fear. Slow things down and put off making permanent decisions until you are more balanced. Try to create short-term, temporary solutions instead of long-term, permanent ones.

Consider what your real values are. Think about what's impor-
tant: security, property, money, revenge, income, peace of mind, your children, cooperative co-parenting, future relationship, doing what's right, being fair, forgiveness, and so on. Attorneys almost always proceed as if getting sole custody and the most money is what's important, but you might have different values and you might prefer your values over the law. Getting every last cent might not be as important to you as other things, like fairness or settlement without legal battle. Or maybe it is.

Consider what your real values are.

If you have trouble reaching decisions, get advice, preferably from a family law attorney who is primarily a mediator (chapter 7). Having organized your facts, you will have pinpointed exactly what you want to know and you can ask the attorney specific and informed questions. Do that, then think things over and decide what you want. But make up your own mind—don't live on someone else's values.

Keep orderly records. Your work will be easier if you keep your records safe, neat, organized, and all together in one place. Otherwise, you may end up swamped in a mass of papers that will make you feel confused, frustrated and insecure. You might misplace important papers. It's easier if you start off right and keep things that way.

Keep file folders in a drawer or box, or go to a stationers and get a large accordion folder with six or more compartments, or just use some large envelopes in a box. Keep a set of files for:

- Correspondence with your spouse, lawyers (if any), and others who are related to your divorce
- Worksheets
- Documents and records
- Any other categories that will help you sort things out

Keep business and personal matters separate

Divorce has a lot of businesslike aspects—money, property, negotiation and agreements—and it is widely understood that business and emotions don't mix well. One of the best things you can do for yourself is to decide to keep business and personal/ emotional matters separate, or as separate as possible. This will make a big contribution toward reducing the level of conflict and confusion in your case and in your own mind. Be sure to tell your spouse what you have decided to do and explain that it will help you both. You can benefit from taking this step unilaterally, but try to get your spouse to agree and set a good precedent by starting off with an agreement that you will both be businesslike. Here are some guidelines:

- Work hard to decide what you want ahead of time. Postpone decisions on things you aren't clear about. Keep a business diary for your thoughts and decisions and review now and then, especially before you go to a meeting.

One of the best things you can do for yourself is to decide to keep business and personal/ emotional matters separate, or as separate as possible.

- Act businesslike. Dress for business instead of casually, adopt a professional attitude and tone of voice. Try to see yourself as two separate people—a business professional and an emotional, feeling human being. Be the other person some other time. Postpone meetings if you cannot be relatively calm and thoroughly prepared.

- Discuss business at appointed times and places. Always be prepared with a written agenda of what you want to talk about and check off each item as it gets done. Bring copies of any necessary documents. Take notes.

- If you meet in person, do not meet at the home of either spouse. It's too personal, it triggers emotions, and someone may feel at a disadvantage. You should be able to get up and leave if necessary. Meet at a coffee shop, in a library or school room, at a park or a friend's house if it feels good. Anywhere quiet, safe and neutral will do, but do not meet at a spouse's home.

- Refuse to discuss business and personal matters in the same conversation. Be consistent and diligent about it. If something personal comes up when talking business, say "I'd like to discuss that later with you, please," and offer to set a specific time for it. If your spouse persists, hold firm, repeat your request once more, then explain that you will leave or hang up if it happens again. If necessary, do so. Don't get excited or emotional; be businesslike, but stick to your decision.

- Refuse to talk business when you are discussing personal matters. Do not get into a business discussion spontaneously or impulsively. You need to be properly prepared and emotionally composed each time.

Try to see yourself as two separate people—a business professional and an emotional, feeling human being. Be the other person some other time.

- If your spouse is being difficult in your emotional life, try not to let that infect your business relationship. Similarly, if your spouse is being bad in business negotiations, don't let that affect you emotionally. Don't get upset—it's only business.

Common traps

Ignorance is the most common trap in the business of divorce. Because your life is upside down you may not want to deal with tedious financial details, but if you don't take the trouble to understand your own financial life, you might as well hang a big "victim" sign around your neck. Ignorance increases your own sense of helplessness and leaves you vulnerable to the risk of being manipulated, of getting a bad deal. You can seek advice and assistance from professionals, but you should never rely on anyone but yourself to take care of business for you. Use the worksheets on the CD that comes with this book to organize and understand your affairs.

Don't get upset— it's only business.

Bad judgment is a real hazard when emotions are running high, but let's face it, divorces are like that. Insecurity makes you doubt your own thinking and ability. Fear and anger make you grasp for too much or surrender too much.

Of course, you should get what you are entitled to, but to demand more for emotional reasons is inviting a ruinous conflict that might leave you with less in the end. Giving up what you have a right to can leave you with a future full of regret if not hardship. So be careful and take precautions against your own emotionally affected judgment:

- Understand the emotional cycles that you and your spouse are going through (chapter 3). Keep in mind that at any given time, emotions can strongly affect your judgment and decision-making.

- Keep business and emotional issues separate (see above).

- Don't jump to sudden conclusions or make impulsive agreements or decisions. Most of all, unless you face an emergency that can't wait, don't rush off to a lawyer until you are informed and prepared and have read step 7.

- Don't sign anything you haven't thought about or don't understand.

- Keep a journal and make entries in it regularly about your thoughts and feelings. Keep track of your evolving priorities, possible solutions to problems, and your goals. Review your journal regularly, especially before making final decisions.

- Use the law as a guide. You are not required to follow the legal standards, but if you are confused or in doubt about what you want to do, and if the laws in your state are clear and predictable, use them as a guide.

- Seek advice from reliable, informed, experienced people.

Don't sign anything you haven't thought about or don't understand.

Excessive spending is very common before, during and after a separation. At first, spending seems like a denial of the growing distance and disaffection between the spouses. A couple will buy a new home or remodel their old one, buy a car, take a long vacation, have a baby—anything to bring them together in *something*. Usually, this is not planned consciously; it just works that way. During separation, spending is used as an anesthetic for emotional pain. After separation, the couple genuinely needs a lot of money to set up two separate life-styles, added to which is neurotic spending driven by emotional upset.

Being aware of this trap might be of some help, but it is often difficult to see and control your own eccentricities. Control impulsive and compulsive buying the same way you would control neurotic eating habits. The best thing is to take every possible step to keep yourself open, centered and strong. Deal directly with your emotional issues instead of reacting and running from them.

Money-hiding is not common but not rare, either. Once it is clear that a divorce is coming, sometimes one spouse or the other will start putting money or other assets aside in a private account or location. If done without cheating the community, this is actually a good idea because it gives that spouse a sense of security. However, if marital assets that belong to both spouses are being secretly diverted into a separate account, this is cheating. A spouse might spend joint savings or take out a loan for living expenses while putting regular income into a separate account; a family business can be manipulated or run down so income appears low; bonuses and commissions can be postponed until after separation—the list is long. Moderate amounts may not be worth fighting over, but it is something to watch out for—see the last page of the Appendix—and include in any future accounting. In extreme cases, you will want an attorney to get court orders to protect the marital estate and your interest in it.

Deal directly with your emotional issues instead of reacting and running from them.

If a divorce is coming, take a careful look at plans to refinance your house or other kind of loan. Watch where income goes and watch your savings account withdrawals. After separation, examine financial transactions during the previous year.

Money management—two households on one income

This may be the most common divorce problem and a powerful source of fear that fuels conflict. Expenses go up dramatically while income stays stable at best and two households now have to live on the same old income. It is the unknown that makes us afraid of the future, afraid of change. What will you live on? How will you make ends meet?

Once your safety is assured, your next most important need is financial security. The difference between a desperate existence and a good life is knowing that you have enough coming in and an emergency reserve that will see you through several months. Living securely on a reduced standard of living is far better than a higher standard of living that is always at risk. Most people don't seem to know this.

Once again, knowledge is power, the best solution. You will solve your money problems by using a budget to help you understand your finances and make plans for the future. When the budget is clear, you will know what you have to do to be secure and live in balance.

Try this seven-point system to solve money problems and plan your future:

- Make an inventory of assets that you own, bills that you owe
- Study your past spending patterns
- Make an inventory of income that you can count on
- Plan your future spending
- Create a control system
- Seek creative alternatives and set goals
- Review and change

Living securely on a reduced standard of living is far better than a higher standard of living that is always at risk.

Make an inventory of property that you own and bills that you owe. Use the Assets and Debts Worksheet on the CD to help you organize and analyze your assets and debts. If you own valuable property after your divorce, you might decide to sell it and use the money for living or for investments. As to debts, any budget you make will have to include a plan to pay them off.

If you become overwhelmed by your debts and repayment makes your budget impossible, you have to consider plans to reorganize your debts. Many areas have organizations such as Consumer Credit Counseling (see the white pages in your phone book), a nonprofit organization that will help you consolidate and repay your debts. Bankruptcy was recently made more difficult, but take a look at the Nolo Press books on bankruptcy at **www.nolo.com** or at your public library.

Study past spending patterns. Use the Budget Worksheet on the CD to organize and analyze spending. Gather all records, bills, receipts, checks and checkbook registers covering at least one year. Some expenses are annual or irregular, so a shorter period might not give you an accurate picture and an unanticipated annual expense (say, several hundred for insurance) could create a crisis. Offer to make copies of records your spouse has and offer to give your spouse copies of records you have. If your spouse won't turn over records you need, a lawyer can force them out through a legal process that in most states is called "discovery."

If your records are incomplete, you will just have to make estimates from memory. By all means, start saving checks and receipts from now on. Use the Budget Worksheet as a guide to keep a precise record of your ongoing expenses over a period of time.

If your income is going to become reduced or uncertain, you may have to start some new habits. Consider it growth, an adventure.

Most people have never analyzed their spending and have never made any organized effort to control it. If your income is going to become reduced or uncertain, you may have to start some new habits. Consider it growth, an adventure.

Make an inventory of income that you can count on. Use the Budget Worksheet. What income can you count on? Naturally, you will need to be very aware of your rights or your obligations regarding child and spousal support. How much can you get? How much will you be expected to pay? What is reasonable? You should also be aware of the possibility that a spouse in need can go immediately into court to ask for temporary support and other orders that will be in effect until a final settlement by agreement or by trial and judgment.

You should figure a low estimate for irregular or uncertain income, because if your actual income is lower, your planning will fail and you will end up in a financial squeeze. Are you counting on support payments? Your chance for actually collecting support payments is higher when spouses reach an agreement, but tougher laws have made payments more reliable when the payer is employed. Laws are increasingly aggressive and tough on people who slack off on their support obligations. But be cautious and realistic about how much you figure to rely on.

Plan your future spending. When you know how your money has been spent in the past, you are in a good position to make an informed estimate of spending needs in the future. Again, use the worksheet. You have to make sure that the spending you plan is no greater than the income you can count on.

Again, use the worksheet. You have to make sure that the spending you plan is no greater than the income you can count on.

If you occasionally earn more than you spend, put some into emergency reserves and investments for future security. Try to accumulate enough savings to live on for several months in case of an emergency. That's the only way to be secure.

If your spending needs exceed the income you can count on, you have only two alternatives: reduce your spending needs or find new sources of reliable income. Living on a lower standard of living is much better than the emotional stress and insecurity of living beyond your means. When cutting expenses, the worst place to compromise is in the food category. Your health comes first, but you can live very nicely on fresh fruits and vegetables, grains, and the occasional fish or chicken. Actually, that's the best possible diet, and it doesn't cost as much as packaged foods, fast foods, and meals out.

If forced to, you can spend savings or sell off assets to raise money, but these are not solutions because you aren't solving your basic problem of more going out than comes in. When you run out, then what do you do?

Create a control system. A budget only works if there is some way to keep track of your spending and keep yourself within its guidelines. You don't need to label every penny, but you do want to watch your spending by budget category. There are a variety of methods you can use:

- Sort your income into envelopes by budget category. You can always see what's left to spend in each envelope and when you run out, you're out. The disadvantage is that you might not want to keep loose cash lying around.

- Keeping a record, like a ledger, of everything you spend works very well, but fails if you let down or forget to enter every expense. This is tedious and requires discipline, but it is the best method in most cases.

- Keep track in your mind. This is simple and works for some people who have simple budgets, but requires discipline and it's easy to make mistakes or fool yourself.

- If you are affluent, hire a financial secretary who receives your income, pays your bills, keeps track of your expenses and gives you a personal allowance.

Create a reserve of emergency funds sufficient for several months.

Seek creative alternatives and set goals. Now that you have a handle on your income and spending, you should set some goals for the future. Be as specific as possible. Very high on your list should be to create a reserve of emergency funds sufficient for several months. Beyond that, you should consider a plan for investing in your future. If your budget is too tight or your income is too low, you will want to find ways to create more reliable income. This means looking for new work, more education and training, new opportunities, a new career. Read books on careers and consider seeing a career counselor.

Review and change. After your system runs for a while, you should sit down and review it carefully to see how it is working. Has anything changed? If so, you need to change your budget. If you can't stay within a category, try to figure out why. Adjust and fine-tune your categories, revise your goals.

Problems? If you find the budget process too difficult, you might want to see a financial or credit counselor. Many areas have an office of Consumer Credit Counselors who will either help you or perhaps refer you to someone who can. Otherwise, you might ask your local bank loan manager or an accountant if they know any professionals who specialize in helping people with budgets.

Whose children will you send to college: yours or some lawyer's?

Step 7. Before you talk to an attorney

Here are some things you need to know before you go see an attorney.

a. How much does a divorce cost? When people ask that question, I always ask, "How much do you have?" I ask, "Whose children will you send to college: yours or some lawyer's?" This is what will happen if you do the worst possible thing and hire an attorney before you are informed and prepared.

b. What a divorce is really about: property, support, parenting. That's all. If you can decide how to divide your marital property and debts, what to do about support, and how to parent your children after separation, then all that's left is paperwork. If your Ex is not likely to come to court to oppose you, you can pretty much get what you want. If your Ex is in the picture and cares what happens, you need to work out an agreement. You do not want to have an attorney contact your Ex or send them letters or start a case before your Ex is prepared and cooperative, otherwise this will surely send them running to get another lawyer involved. Then you'll have *four* people who can't talk to each other and the level of upset will go up, it will take more time and cost a lot more.

c. Divorce problems and inability to agree on terms are almost never about the law, almost always about personalities and emotional upset.

d. Neither the law nor attorneys who work in the law have tools to help solve divorce problems. In fact, the legal system and the way attorneys work is almost certain to make things worse. The legal system is based on conflict, arguing before a judge in order to win. You don't want more argument, you want less. Arguing doesn't settle anything. The legal route doesn't work, takes too long, costs too much, and leaves the parties wrung out and broke.

The things you can do to help yourself are far superior to anything an attorney can do.

e. The things you can do to help yourself are far superior to anything an attorney can do. When self-help isn't enough, you don't want an attorney, you want a mediator.

f. At some point, you might want some information about the law from an attorney, but that's all—advice. Unless you face an emergency, you do not want to hire an attorney to take your case because he/she will surely make things worse and, even then, you can consider hiring the attorney just for one purpose, like getting restraining orders or temporary orders for child custody and support. Some will do this, some won't. Shop around. If you do go to an attorney for advice, don't go until you have your facts in order and know exactly what you want from the attorney.

g. Before an attorney can answer questions, he or she will need to know all the details about your case: dates of marriage and separation, your kids, your income and expenses, your property and debts. Why pay for a lot of time having an attorney explain this to you and getting the facts from you? Show up with all your facts written down and clearly presented. Our worksheets (on the CD) help you develop and organize your facts in the same way an attorney would and you can do it yourself for free. You have to do it eventually, anyway, in order to get through your divorce, so you might as well start now.

h. Know what you want from the attorney. You don't want to retain the attorney to take over your case, but you might want some questions answered. Write these down ahead of time so you can make sure they all get covered. The problem is to find an attorney who will give you advice in plain English without making it all seem too difficult to handle without the attorney. This is very common.

Know what you want from the attorney.

Step 8. Before you talk about divorce with your spouse

This chapter is about cases where both spouses are present and in disagreement about the terms of the divorce—from simple difference of opinion to active upset and anger. As you will see here, the things you can do yourself are far more effective than anything a lawyer can do. I am addressing a very wide range of possible situations here, so use whatever seems useful for your own situation.

Abusive spouse. If your spouse is an abuser/controller, you can read this chapter for ideas, but you might need specialized counseling and assistance and you might need to establish a position of strength and security with restraining orders and other steps. Read chapters 1E, 5 and 9.

Over 95% of all cases are settled before they get to trial, so your case is very likely to settle, too. Unfortunately, too many cases are settled only after the spouses have spent their financial and emotional resources on lawyers and legal battle. The time and effort spent battling will have impaired their ability to get on with their lives and may have caused serious psychic damage to themselves and their children. These couples could have saved themselves all that simply by agreeing to settle earlier. So, why didn't they?

The five obstacles to agreement

In fact, there are some very good reasons why it's hard for spouses to work out an agreement—five, to be exact:

Over 95% of all cases are settled before they get to trial, so your case is very likely to settle, too.

- Emotional upset and conflict
- Insecurity and fear
- Ignorance and misinformation
- The legal system and lawyers, and finally
- Real disagreement

To get an agreement, in or out of the system, with or without an attorney, you have to overcome these five obstacles. Let's look at them in a little more detail.

1. **Emotional upset and conflict.** This is about high levels of anger, hurt, blame, and guilt—a very normal part of divorce. If one or both spouses are upset, you can't negotiate, have reasonable discussions or make sound decisions. Volatile emotions become externalized and attached to things or to the children. When emotions are high, reason is at its lowest ebb and will not be very effective at that time. There are various causes of upset:

   - The divorce itself, stress of major change, broken dreams, fear of change, fear of an unknown future

- Lack of mutual acceptance of the divorce and willingness to separate—sometimes the biggest obstacle of all

- History of bad communication habits or conflict

- Particular events or circumstances (a new lover, a new debt)

2. **Insecurity, fear, unequal bargaining power.** You can't negotiate if either spouse feels incompetent, afraid, or believes the other spouse has some big advantage. Divorce is tremendously undermining and tends to multiply any general lack of self-confidence and self-esteem. Also, there are often very real causes for insecurity: lack of skill and experience at dealing with business and negotiation, and lack of complete information and knowledge about the process and the marital affairs. It doesn't matter if insecurity is real or reasonable; it is real if it feels real.

3. **Ignorance and misinformation.** Ignorance about the legal system and how it works can make you feel uncertain, insecure and incompetent. You feel as if you don't know what you are doing—and you are right. Misinformation is when the things you think you know are not correct. Misinformation comes from friends, television, movies, even from lawyers who are not family law specialists. It can distort your expectations about your rights and what's fair. It's hard to negotiate with someone who has mistaken ideas about what the rules are. Fortunately, both conditions can be easily fixed with *reliable* information.

4. **The legal system and lawyers.** We've discussed this at length. It does not help you overcome obstacles to agreement but, rather it is one of the major obstacles that you have to overcome. You want to avoid the legal system as much as possible—and you can.

You want to avoid the legal system as much as possible—and you can.

5. **Real disagreement.** Real disagreements are valid differences based on the fact that the spouses now have different needs and interests. After dealing with the first four obstacles, these valid issues might turn out to be minor, but even if serious, at least they can be negotiated rationally.

The solutions are in your hands. Apart from the legal system—which you can avoid—all obstacles to your agreement are personal, between you and your spouse and between you and yourself. The solutions are entirely in your own hands and the legal system has little to offer compared with the potential for harm, and especially compared with all the things you can do for yourself outside the legal system.

You need to arrange things so both spouses are comfortable about not retaining an attorney.

Take care. Emotional upset, especially insecurity and fear, is what drives people into lawyers' offices. Try to avoid doing anything that might increase the upset and fear of either spouse. The upset person is saying, "I can't stand this, I won't take it anymore! I'm going to get a lawyer!" The insecure person is saying, "I can't understand all this, I can't deal with it, I can't deal with my spouse. I want to be safe. I need someone to help me. I'm going to get a lawyer." And this is how cases get dragged into unnecessary legal conflict.

You need to arrange things so both spouses are comfortable about not retaining an attorney. If you think your spouse may be upset or insecure, you have to be very careful and patient. If you are feeling incapable of dealing with your own divorce, the information in this book will help a lot and you will see that you can get all the help and support you need without retaining an attorney.

How to overcome the five obstacles to agreement

You want to work on your agreement outside the legal system, because the things you can do to help yourself are far more effective than anything a lawyer can do for you. At whatever point you decide that you can't work things out on your own, you still don't need an attorney, you need a mediator. But first, there are things you can and should do to help things along. Follow these steps, one after the other.

Read chapter 3F again, *How to reduce conflict and stress.* You'll find some or all of those techniques very useful, helping you set the stage for negotiation. Taking the steps up to this point will help calm things down. This means you have established a period of safe stability for yourself at least for a while, you are protecting your children (if any), and you've done what you can to help your spouse get safe and stable for a while. You've taken advice only from reliable sources, organized your facts and got reliable answers to questions you might have about the laws of your state, so you pretty much know what you think is fair. You've slowed yourself down and worked at finding calmness and patience within yourself.

Consider counseling or therapy for yourself or your children.

Temporary arrangements. During the early days of your separation, if you two can work out your own temporary arrangements for paying the bills and parenting the children, neither of you will need an attorney to go to court for temporary orders. Read step 5.

Get help if you need it. Consider counseling or therapy for yourself or your children. For help with talking to your spouse, consider couples counseling or go see a mediator. These low-conflict professionals can help with emotional issues, defusing upset or, in the case of the mediator, with reaching temporary arrangements and permanent agreements.

(continued on page 121)

HOW TO DEAL WITH PASSIVE RESISTANCE

THE TEN STEPS are about dealing with disagreement based on upset, but passive resistance requires a different approach from cases where anger is open and direct. This is where your spouse does not deal with anger directly but engages in non-aggressive behavior that frustrates and obstructs—things like procrastination, stubbornness, sullenness, inefficiency, sarcasm, even malicious gossip. Things never get done, negotiations don't get anywhere, agreements don't get made, you can't move forward. This behavior is very frustrating and can really wear you down.

Wait! Who is doing what to whom? Just because your spouse drags things out and resists the divorce does not by itself mean this is passive resistance. It could be your spouse simply doesn't want the divorce—doesn't want to mediate, nego-tiate, or litigate, but would rather work on saving the marriage. You would deal with this differently than a true passive resister because it's not about concealed anger, it's about love and attachment. If your spouse has not typically been a passive resister in the past, your spouse prob-ably is not one now. You need to consider your own role and maybe work together in counseling until you both understand and accept the direction things will take, one way or the other. Doing this will take

some time, but it's worth it—far superior to forcing your case into litigation.

If it's real, if you have a true case of passive resistance, keep your cool and be patient. Don't reward your spouse by letting it show that his/her behavior is bothering you. Recognize that the behavior is based on concealed anger or resentment and deal with it as such. Tell your spouse you understand that he/she is hurt and angry and that you feel sorry for that, but it would be better for both of you if it could be dealt with directly. Communicate in person or in writing (better not to use email), but keep communicating at each stage.

Here are some suggestions. You know your spouse better than anyone, so you are in the best position to decide how to deal with him/her. These are suggestions for you to think about, but you have to decide how best to move forward.

1. If you say you are going to do something—move out, empty an account, fill out papers, file the divorce, whatever—always follow through and do it. Don't reward passive resistant behavior.

2. Tell your spouse your mind is made up, the divorce is going to happen anyway, but it would save a lot of

money that you can both use if you could work things out in a fair agreement rather than end up in court. But either way, you are going forward.

3. Show signs of going forward yourself. Show your spouse the papers that you are working on in order to get your divorce started. Give him/her a copy of this book and discuss ideas in it.

4. Take small steps and offer options at each step. Say things like, I'm reading this book about the best way to do our divorce—would you like to see it? I'm getting the papers to fill out tomorrow. I'm going to start filling them out, if you'd like to discuss it. Would you like to discuss terms with a mediator? I'm going to file the papers tomorrow and you'll be served. Would you like to discuss the terms? If we don't get an agreement, I'm go to proceed to the next step, would you like to discuss it? And so on.

5. Keep repeating calmly that the divorce is going to happen with or without cooperation and that it is probably best for both of you (and the kids if you have any) if you can agree to mediate or negotiate the terms together. You'd like to arrange terms that you both feel are comfortable but you are not willing to wait indefinitely. Set some reasonable deadlines for your small steps and then go on to the next step.

6. Set deadlines for your steps. Say that if you are not making progress by a certain date (a few weeks), you won't wait for an agreement but will file a petition for divorce and start it without one.

7. Read chapter 8 and find out how to file divorce papers yourself or with help. Be prepared so when it's time to move forward, you'll be ready. Prepare your papers so you can file them if there has been no progress by the deadline. You don't want surprises, so tell your spouse you've filed for a divorce and that it will soon be served, then go ahead and get it done.

8. File your petition and have it served on your spouse. Before papers are served, send a letter stating that you have been trying to minimize the use of attorneys so you can keep most of what you have rather than wasting a lot of money unnecessarily on attorneys. State that you will always remain open to negotiation or mediation to get matters settled and would prefer it. Give your spouse a copy of this book or the address to my web site at **www.nolodivorce.com**.

9. Serve the first papers with a letter promising that you won't take the next step without giving 30 days written notice of your intention to move forward. Say, "This promise is legally binding and I give it so you will not feel any pressure to file an answer or response and to give us time to start working on an agreement ourselves or in mediation. I promise that I won't push the legal case as long as we are making some progress on our agreement."

10. If this doesn't produce movement, or if things bog down unreasonably, tell your spouse you are going to give the written notice in a week if there's no progress, then send your spouse a letter announcing that in 30 days you intend to file additional papers to move the legal case forward. Then do it.

11. Pushing the paperwork forward means that you will soon find out if you're going to end up with an easy or difficult divorce. If your spouse doesn't file papers in court to oppose you, your case will be easy. If your spouse gets an attorney or finds some other way to file a response, you'll have a contested case.

Things can now go three ways:

- Your spouse starts to cooperate and you work your way toward an agreement.

- Your spouse stays passive and does not oppose you in court so you end up with an easy divorce. The problem is that you won't know if the plan is working until the time limit for filing papers has expired and you formally move to the next stage.

- Your spouse gets an attorney, still trying to obstruct the divorce. This third outcome is not good, but at least things are moving. If this happens, you can try negotiating directly with the attorney or you can hire your own attorney to help to get your case set for trial and move it toward a judgment.

If you find yourself in a legal battle, join our Battle Group. Read chapter 9. Always keep the door open to negotiation and mediation. Keep offering to make an appointment to mediate.

Step 9. How to negotiate with your spouse

The best predictor of a good divorce outcome is client rather than attorney control of negotiation. This doesn't mean you should not get help and advice from an attorney when you want it, it means you are better off if you can do most or all of the negotiating yourself. This is also realistic because studies indicate that clients feel their attorneys don't actually give them much help or guidance anyway. Studies have revealed that nearly half of all divorce clients reported no more than three contacts with their attorney, *including* phone calls, while 60% said they had worked out all issues without attorney help. In cases with children where both spouses had attorneys, less than 20% felt their lawyers played a major role in settlement negotiations. So, you are likely to end up dealing with the negotiation anyway, and there is strong evidence that you are far better off if you do. You get a higher degree of compliance with terms of agreement, a much lower chance for future courtroom conflict, and a lot more general good will. This is especially important if you have children and co-parenting to consider.

You are better off if you can do most or all of the negotiating yourself.

Here are ten steps that will help make negotiating with your spouse smoother and more effective.

1. **Be businesslike.** Keep business and personal matters separate. You can talk about personal matters any time, but never discuss business without an appointment and an agenda. This is so you can both be prepared and composed. Read step 6 again where I discussed this topic in detail.

   Act businesslike. Be on time and dress for business. Don't socialize and don't drink—it impairs your judgment.

   Be polite and insist on reasonable manners in return. If things start to sneak into the personal or become un-businesslike, say you're going to stop if the meeting doesn't get back on track. Ask to set another date. If matters don't improve, don't argue, don't get mad, just get up and go. Wave goodbye and say, "Lets think about this and schedule another meeting, okay?" If it continues, read the side article about dealing with passive resistance found on page 118.

2. **Meet on neutral ground.** Don't meet at the home or office of either spouse where there could be too many reminders, memories, personal triggers. The visiting spouse could feel at a disadvantage and the home spouse can't get up and go if things get out of hand. Try a nearby church, a quiet and private restaurant booth, the park, borrow a meeting space or rent one if necessary.

If you feel insecure, become informed, be well prepared, use an agenda, get expert advice and guidance.

3. **Be prepared.** Get control of the facts of your own divorce (see the Appendix); understand how the laws of your state apply to the facts; find out the probable outcomes under the law; clarify your goals. You can also prepare by trying to understand your respective emotions and past patterns. Just the fact that you are trying to do this will help make things a little better. If you're going to get legal advice about how the laws in your state apply to your case, do it before you start to negotiate. You can also take time off from any stage of the negotiation to get more advice on any specific point that comes up.

4. **Balance the negotiating power.** If you feel insecure, become informed, be well prepared, use an agenda, get expert advice and guidance. You never need to respond to any issue on the spot: state your ideas, listen to your spouse, then think about it until the next meeting. Use friends for moral support and venting (but not advice), then go back in there. Don't meet if you are not calm; don't continue if the meeting doesn't stay businesslike. Consider using a professional mediator.

If you are stronger or better informed, help build your spouse's confidence so he/she can negotiate competently and make sound decisions. Share all information openly. Be a good listener—restate what your spouse says to show you heard it and don't respond immediately, just say you'll think about it. Tone yourself back, state your own points clearly but don't try to persuade or "win" a point. Don't argue or repeat yourself. Listen, listen, listen.

5. **Focus on needs and interests, don't take positions.** A position is a stand on a final outcome: "I want the house sold and the children every weekend." In the beginning, there's too much upset and too little information to decide what you want in the end, and positions are a trigger for argument because the other side either agrees or disagrees. It's far better to think and talk about needs and interests. For example: "I want what's fair and what the rules say is mine; I need to be secure and have enough to live on; I want to know what I can count on for living expenses; I want maximum contact with my children; I'd like the kids to stay in the same school district; I need to get out of debt, especially on credit cards; I want an end to argument and upset." These are goals that you can discuss together.

Compromise makes sense, because if you can't prove some fact to each other, you'd have a hard time proving it in court.

6. **Build agreement.** Start with the facts. By now you should have gathered and exchanged all information. If not, complete this step then try to agree what the facts are. Write down the facts you agree on and list exactly what facts you do not agree on. Note any competing versions then do research to find documents or other evidence that will resolve differences. Or compromise. Compromise makes sense, because if you can't prove some fact to each other, you'd have a hard time proving it in court.

Make a list of the issues and decisions you can agree on. Write them down. This is how you build a foundation for agreement and begin to clarify the major issues between you. Next, write down the things you don't agree on, always trying to refine your differences—to make them more and more clear and precise. Try to break differences down into digestible, bite-sized pieces. Keep another list of information you need to gather or look up, or advice you intend to get.

7. **State issues in a constructive way.** Reframing is when you re-state things in a more neutral way, to encourage communication and understanding. For example: One spouse says, "I have to have the house." Reframe: "What I would like most is to have the house, that's my first priority. What the house means to me is..."

8. **Get legal advice.** Legal questions often come up as you negotiate. Get advice. Find out if the laws of your state provide a predictable outcome on your particular issues. Don't hesitate to get more than one opinion. See chapter 7 for who to call.

9. **Be patient and persistent.** Don't rush, don't be in a hurry. Divorces take time and negotiation takes time. Whenever someone hears a new idea, it takes time to percolate. It takes time for people to change their minds. It may take time to shift your mutual orientation from combative to competitive to cooperative. So don't just *do* something; *stand* there! A slow, gradual approach takes pressure off and allows emotions to cool. Meanwhile, you might want to work out temporary solutions for certain issues. If the situation of both spouses is stable and secure for a while, you can afford to take some time. If not, work on that, not the negotiation. Settle in, get as comfortable as you can, go on with building your new life. If the going seems slow, remember, working through attorneys usually takes a very long time, many months or even years. You can beat that, for sure.

A slow, gradual approach takes pressure off and allows emotions to cool.

10. **Get help.** Negotiating with your spouse may not be easy; you're dealing with old habits, raw wounds, entrenched personality patterns—all the obstacles to agreement all at once. A third person can really help keep things in focus. Mediators are professionals who are specially trained to help you negotiate; they are expert at helping couples get unblocked and into an agreement. Mediation is very effective and usually takes only a few sessions. **Advice.** It can often help to get advice on how laws of your state apply to your facts. Read chapter 7, *I want someone to help me—Who can I call?* In California, you can call Divorce Helpline at (800) 359-7004 for help with your negotiation; it's one of the many things they do very well.

The three befores. If you do get help, be sure to get legal information and advice *before* you state your position to your spouse, *before* you draft your settlement agreement, and *before* you sign anything.

If you do get help, be sure to get legal information and advice before you state your position to your spouse, before you draft your settlement agreement, and before you sign anything.

Before you begin to negotiate, give your spouse this book and, if possible, discuss parts of it together. Talk about how you can put these ideas to work and how you can proceed. Go over each step and talk about how it's going and what more can be done. There are many good books about negotiation, but one of the easiest to read is the little Penguin paperback by Fisher and Ury, *Getting to Yes: Negotiating Agreement Without Giving In*. The chapter titles are a checklist for things you need to know:

- Don't bargain over positions
- Separate the people from the problem
- Focus on interests, not positions
- Invent options for mutual gain
- Insist on using objective criteria
- What if they are more powerful?
- What if they won't play?
- What if they use dirty tricks?

After you agree. Chances are very good that you can work things out by using the methods discussed in this book. Once you have reached an agreement, you can relax a little bit, your divorce is effectively over—all that's left is to get it drafted in legally correct form and then go through some red tape and paperwork to get your judgment. Read about how to do this in chapter 8.

If you can't agree. If you find that working on an agreement isn't getting anywhere, don't struggle too long, don't wait until you are both at war from entrenched positions, don't get frustrated, don't get depressed, don't get mad—get help. If you can't work well together or can't get an agreement, you don't need a lawyer, you need a mediator. Read chapter 7, *I want someone to help me—Who can I call?* Read about what mediators do and how to choose one.

The settlement agreement is virtually your entire divorce and your future life.

Step 10. How to put your agreement in writing

Once all issues are settled and you have an outline of what you have agreed to do about property, support and (if you have kids) parenting, a written agreement now needs to be drafted in a legally sufficient form. You can do it yourself or get help, so consider each of the four methods described below.

How much is good help worth? The settlement agreement is virtually your entire divorce and your future life. Is it worth it to get professional help? Add up the value of all property and debts then add all future support payments. Compare that to the few hundred it costs to get professional help and a settlement agreement that is done right. If you have equity in real estate or significant amounts in retirement funds, you should have your agreement drafted by an attorney.

a) **Do it yourself.** If expert help isn't worth it, or you prefer to do it yourself anyway, use the sample agreement on our CD as a guide. Because there are 50 states with different rules and thousands of counties and judicial districts, each with different judges, some courts will have their own ideas about how an agreement should be written. For example, California has very specific and unique requirements for how spouses must give disclosure to one another before signing an agreement, so in California or Texas you should use the sample agreement found in the book *How to Do Your Own Divorce*. You should have both signatures notarized when you sign your own settlement agreement. This is not expensive and while it is required only in some courts it is a good idea in every case

Once you've drafted and signed your settlement agreement, go ahead and submit it with your other divorce paperwork and if it gets sent back, they will either say why so you can fix it, or you can go to Plan B and take it to a local attorney for drafting and submit it again.

b) **DealMaker Settlement Agreement Software.** I created this very powerful, sophisticated and ridiculously inexpensive program, good in all states, to help you draft a professional settlement agreement. DealMaker guides you through entering information and making decisions, then drafts a comprehensive agreement ready to edit, or sign it as it is. To learn more and get a free trial version, go to **www.nolodivorce.com/US.**

c) **Get a document service to do it.** In any state, you can look for a legal document preparation service that works under the supervision of an attorney who will draft or review your agreement. Or, if you find a document service, financial planner or accountant who uses my DealMaker Pro Settlement Agreement software, that would be another good option.

d) **Get an attorney to draft it.** Go to a family law attorney— preferably one who does a lot of divorce mediation—and

Because there are 50 states with different rules and thousands of counties and judicial districts, each with different judges, some courts will have their own ideas about how an agreement should be written.

Once you have a written settlement agreement, you now have an Easy Divorce.

ask how much it will cost to draft a settlement agreement that is already worked out and agreed to by both parties. Shop around for prices. Do not let a non-attorney (paralegal or typing service) draft your agreement unless they are supervised by an attorney who reviews all agreements or unless you have very little property and not much to lose.

Resolution of disputes. Whoever writes your agreement, make sure it has a clause near the end, "Resolution of Disputes," where you agree that with the exception of emergencies involving imminent threat to the safety of either party or their minor children, or the collection of back support, if any disagreements arise between you in the future on any other issues, you will resolve them by mediation. This language is found in our sample agreement and in Nolo's DealMaker settlement agreement software.

What's next?

Once you have a written settlement agreement, you now have an Easy Divorce. All you need now is some paperwork to get your divorce judgment. Read chapter 8, *How to do your own divorce.*

Get my Free Divorce Checklist. There are practical things you should do and things you should know. Some are best done before the divorce is even announced, some will be easier before you separate, but all should be done as soon as you can manage. It's free at **www.nolodivorce.com/RR**.

7

I WANT SOMEONE TO HELP ME
– Who can I call?

IF YOU MAKE GOOD USE OF THIS BOOK, you might not need help, but for sure you will need less of it and you will know what kind of help you want and how to find it.

Who you call depends on what kind of help you want. Sections A–C suggest who you can call and the services they offer. Section D is organized around the kind of help you want and who best to call for your needs.

Who you call depends on what kind of help you want.

A. Friends and relatives
B. Legal documents preparers (typists, paralegals)
C. Attorneys

- Mediators
- Collaborative lawyers
- Limited representation
- Divorce Helpline
- Aggressive litigation

D. Help with what?
E. How to shop for a professional
F. How to fire your attorney

A. Friends and relatives

This is your least reliable source of advice. Take all the moral support you can get, but when you get advice about how to handle your case, smile and say "Thank you," but keep in mind that they might be dead wrong. However well-meaning, family and friends are often misinformed and for sure they lack a professional's depth and breadth of knowledge.

If you didn't get it from my books or a *reliable* family law attorney, don't trust it! Just because you like or trust someone doesn't make them right. If you take bad advice, you are the one who pays the price, so be careful.

If you take bad advice, you are the one who pays the price, so be careful.

B. Legal document services (typists, paralegals)

If you know pretty much how you want to settle your marital affairs, and if you don't need legal advice or problem solving or help with writing a settlement agreement, and if you are very sure your spouse will not file papers in court to oppose your divorce action, then perhaps all you need is help with typing and processing the legal documents that will get you a judgment (or decree) of divorce (or dissolution).

Non-attorneys who offer legal forms services directly to the public go by different names from state to state. Here, we'll call them Legal Document Assistants (LDAs), but you might find them listed in yellow pages as:

> Divorce Assistance
> Document Preparation Service
> Legal Clinics
> Legal Documents Assistants (or Preparers)
> Legal Services
> Paralegals
> Typing Service
> Word Processing Service

California cases. We keep a very active directory of professionals who will help you do your own divorce on our web site at **www. nolodivorce.com/dir**.

Other states. Look in your local yellow pages under the categories listed above.

In theory, you tell a legal document assistant what information you want typed and on which forms, then they type them up and do the secretarial work. In practice, they provide more guidance. Rates range from $200 to $800 or more for divorce paperwork. We introduced this innovation in legal service in 1973 and it has since changed the face of the legal map across the United States, saving consumers billions of dollars.

No education or training is required to be an LDA, but in some states they have created professional associations that offer training and certification. For example, the California Association of Legal Document Assistants (**www.calda.org**) offers its members training and promotes high standards in education, ethics and business practices. We are a Sustaining Member of CALDA.

LDAs cannot give you reliable legal advice, nor should you have one write your settlement agreement unless they using my DealMaker software or are working with an attorney who reviews the work. Just as when hiring a lawyer or a mechanic, be careful who you hire. Ask how long he/she has been in business and check references! Read section E below for tips on how to find a professional.

Just as when hiring a lawyer or a mechanic, be careful who you hire.

C. Attorneys

California cases. No need to read further. Call Divorce Helpline at (800) 359-7004 to talk to a top quality family law attorney who will act as your coach or guide, help solve problems, develop options, talk to your spouse, mediate, arbitrate, settle, write your agreement and do all paperwork to get your judgment. They serve the entire state by phone or at their offices across the state. I founded this company in 1990 and left it in 2007. Although I am no longer a part of Divorce Helpline, I know all of the attorneys personally and trust them completely. They are extremely useful, effective and affordable.

Taking your divorce to an attorney before you know what you are doing is the worst thing you can do—a well-trod path into escalating conflict. So, unless you have an emergency like those discussed in chapter 5B, it will be much better if you do not retain an attorney until you read this book through chapter 6, step 7.

What kind of attorney? Attorneys take a variety of approaches to divorce that determine how they will handle your case if you call on them for help.

Taking your divorce to an attorney before you know what you are doing is the worst thing you can do—a well-trod path into escalating conflict.

- **A mediator** specializes in helping couples work out an agreement that they can both accept and live by. Many attorneys claim to mediate, but you want a family law attorney who is *primarily* a mediator, one who does little or no litigation. If the issues of your case are limited to personal discord and parenting, there are excellent non-attorney mediators who are probably less expensive, but if your case involves money, property or support, you'd be better off with an attorney mediator who can bring knowledge of state law and local judges into the discussion. Ask if they do that, because many mediators won't do this, preferring each party to have separate counsel, something that greatly increases your cost.

- **Collaborative law attorneys** represent you and speak for you, but they enter into a written agreement with the other side, promising not to go to court or threaten to go to court, concentrating on negotiation and mediation. Depending on your case, they call in an accountant, therapist, child specialist, or financial planner to assist. This approach only works if attorneys on *both* sides are willing to enter into the arrangement. Collaborative divorce has a good track record and even with all the professional services, it will still cost less than a court battle. This is a new but rapidly growing subspecialty, so it is not certain there will be collaborative lawyers near you. Go on the Internet and search "collaborative law" plus the name of your state, or call the local Bar association or other attorneys and ask if they know of any collaborative divorce lawyers near you. When you talk to one, find out how many other such cases they have conducted.

- **Limited representation.** A small but growing number of lawyers are offering representation limited to specific tasks or portions of your case while you keep overall responsibility. For example, they will draft your agreement, or file and appear on one motion. This is not available everywhere, but it is becoming more common. If you want a bit of advice or service from a family law attorney, ask if they offer "limited representation" or "unbundling."

- **Aggressive litigation**. A litigator takes your case to court and plays aggressive hardball to win. By definition, this means arguing with the other side, threatening legal action, and filing motions and battling in court. Most attorneys take this approach but most are not good at it and don't give good service or good value. It's hard to find top quality, even if you pay top dollar. Most have too many cases and too little time, so after the initial interview, don't expect a lot of personal attention, good customer service, or your phone calls returned promptly. Read E below for advice on how to find a litigator.

In really bad cases where you are already under attack or where you are sure your spouse will do something

Collaborative divorce has a good track record and even with all the professional services, it will still cost less than a court battle.

underhanded, a litigator might be what you need, but if you are looking for balanced advice that might lead to peaceful (inexpensive) solutions to your problems, this is not the kind of attorney you want to consult.

D. Help with what?

- **Advice.** To understand your legal rights, practical options, how to solve problems and figure out the best thing to do next, look for a family law attorney who specializes primarily or entirely in mediation. This way, the advice you get will more likely be oriented toward solving problems rather than fighting in court. For California cases, the best thing you can do is call Divorce Helpline, (800) 359-7004.

To understand your legal rights, practical options, how to solve problems and figure out the best thing to do next, look for a family law attorney who specializes primarily or entirely in mediation.

Attorneys will frequently do the first interview for a fairly small fee or nothing at all, but too often they spend that time convincing you that you need to retain them to handle your case rather than giving you useful answers to your questions. Getting practical, useful information and advice from attorneys without retaining them can be tricky, because they don't really want to help you help yourself, they want to be retained to do it all because that's where the big money is—your big money. You do not want to retain an attorney unless you have no other choice. Read chapter 6 through step 7 before you call an attorney.

When you interview attorneys, shopping for the person you want to work with, explain that you primarily want someone to give you information and advice that will lead to a negotiated or mediated settlement, that you do not want to be represented yet or take your case to court at this time. See what they say.

- **Court orders** for support or child custody and visitation or to freeze all financial transfers. Getting orders from court automatically takes your case into battle mode from which it is hard to get back out. But if you are sure there is no other way to work out some temporary arrangements, or if you are sure your spouse will do something underhanded, then it might be necessary to go quickly to court for temporary orders. Look for a family law attorney who does a lot of mediation but also some litigation and try to work into mediation mode as soon as possible.

- **Battle.** If you are sure from the beginning that you won't be able to avoid a fight, you'll be shopping for a litigator—an attorney who fights cases in court and plays hard to win. But litigation is so stressful, destructive, time consuming and terribly expensive that you should read through the steps to see all the things you can do to avoid a legal battle. If you end up going to court, read chapter 9, *How to win a legal battle* to learn how to protect yourself and your children and how to make the best of a very difficult situation.

The best way to find professional help is by personal reputation.

E. How to shop for a professional

The best way to find professional help is by personal reputation. Licenses and certificates are important but do not guarantee that the practitioner will be good or the right person for you. Here are some approaches you can use:

- Try to get a recommendation from someone reliable. Talk to other professionals in related fields or call local divorce support groups. Look in the yellow pages under Divorce Assistance, Attorneys, Mediators, or Counselors.

- Interview more than one prospective professional.

- Ask about their fees, their training and background. Are they licensed? How long have they been in business? Do they do it full time?

- Ask about their area of expertise, what their goals are and what approach they would use in cases like yours.

- **Lawyers.** Strangely, most lawyers do *not* tailor plans for any particular case; rather, they tend to approach all cases in more or less the same way. If you want an attorney to represent you in court, after you've discussed your facts, be sure to ask them what plan or strategy they would recommend for your case. If they don't have one or if what they say does not seem specifically tailored to your case, keep shopping.

The person you work with has to feel right.

- For attorneys, ask if they are willing to give you information and advice without taking your case on retainer, if they offer limited representation or practice collaborative law.

- Do they ask you questions, too, to find out if their service and style is the most appropriate for you?

- Does their work place feel calm and private?

- Do they discuss your options with you?

Finally, the most important thing is not a rational process at all. The person you work with has to feel right. Mediation, counseling, and litigation are intensely personal. Whatever it is that works happens on the level of personalities—yours and theirs. You need to find a professional with strength of character, experience, wisdom, and a personality that suits you. Don't hire someone you are not comfortable with.

F. How to fire your attorney

In most cases, it would be better to get help from an attorney without actually retaining him or her to represent you, that is, to "take" your case and act on your behalf in your divorce. Far better if you pay for whatever advice or limited service you decide you need. But it often happens that people retain an attorney and later find out that they are not getting good service.

You have a right to discharge your attorney at any time for any reason or no reason at all, and whether or not any money is owed. Even if you do, your attorney cannot hold your files but must hand them over immediately to you or to your new attorney.

If your lawyer is not performing to your satisfaction, you may want to send a letter (keep copies) setting out very specifically what needs to be changed. If there is no improvement, start shopping for another lawyer. Some things can't be changed: for example, if you lose trust and confidence in your lawyer, get another one or take over the case yourself. Nothing is worse than feeling trapped in a bad relationship with your own attorney.

You have a right to discharge your attorney at any time for any reason or no reason at all.

If your spouse has an attorney, it would be unwise to fire your old attorney until you have another. However, if your spouse has no attorney, you can consider taking over the case yourself.

New attorney? If you hire a new attorney, your new attorney will file required forms and arrange to get your files from your old attorney.

Taking the case yourself. If you discharge your attorney to take over yourself, do it in writing and keep a copy of the letter. If the attorney has filed documents in court, you must also file a Discharge of Attorney form naming yourself as the new attorney "In Pro Per" or "Pro Se," which means that you represent yourself.

An attorney cannot ethically delay turning over files and documents merely to pressure you into payment of amounts owed.

A Discharge of Attorney form that should work in most states is on the companion CD in the back of this book. There is also a form that is specifically for California. Your court clerk can tell you if there is a local or state form for your court.

Fill out the form, print it, sign it, and make three copies. Have someone (not you) mail a copy to your ex-attorney, your spouse and your spouse's attorney, if any. That person signs the Proof of Service then you file it with the court clerk. Send a letter to your ex-attorney politely explaining that you have taken over your own case and request that all files and papers be immediately forwarded to you.

Your former attorney's duties. An attorney cannot ethically delay turning over files and documents merely to pressure you into payment of amounts owed. Failure to promptly forward files as you request is a breach of the attorney's ethical duty to you. In case of unreasonable delay, fire off a letter of complaint to the local and state Bar associations with copies to your old attorney. Meanwhile, you can always get copies of court documents from the court clerk.

8

HOW TO DO YOUR OWN DIVORCE

IF YOU HAVE A CASE where your spouse won't go to court and oppose you, whether because he/she is gone, doesn't care or can't be bothered, or because you two have been able to work out an agreement regarding property, support and (if there are children) parenting, then getting your judgment is just a matter of some paperwork and red tape. There are several inexpensive ways you can get this done.

Many cases start out unopposed, but it's never a surprise if a case flares up.

A. How to keep an easy case easy

Many cases start out unopposed, but it's never a surprise if a case flares up. Apart from being considerate and sensitive, like not flaunting a new affair or pushing his/her buttons, there are things you can do if your relationship starts to heat up. You deal with flare-ups by taking the same steps I advised to quiet and settle a case that starts out conflicted. These are covered in chapters 3F and 6, where I discuss things you can do to reduce conflict.

Give your spouse a copy of this book—it can only help. That way, you will both have good information and maybe you can talk about things that concern you in terms of the ideas and solutions suggested here.

B. Doing your own divorce

What we've been talking about throughout this book is doing your own divorce. You've already been doing it; you are doing it right now. Doing your own divorce does not mean filling out divorce forms, though you can choose to do that if you want to. It does not mean typing up your own agreement, though you may be able to do that, too, if you have a relatively simple estate and follow the sample agreement on the CD that comes with this book. What is important is that you work out your own terms outside the legal system without retaining an attorney to take over your case. That's doing your own divorce.

The more you can do yourselves, the better off you will be—and that's a scientifically proven fact.

Studies have shown that a good divorce outcome is related to the degree of involvement and participation of both spouses. The more you can do yourselves, the better off you will be—and that's a scientifically proven fact.

Once it's clear that your case will be uncontested, the mechanics of doing a divorce are relatively simple. You may well wonder why lawyers charge so much for doing them. If you take care of things yourself, even if you hire help, you'll be better off and save money and reduce the chance of getting tangled up in the legal system.

There are two kinds of cases that can be handled as uncontested:

- If, at any point in the legal process, you and your spouse reach an agreement on all issues; or

- You don't have an agreement but there'll be no legal opposition from your spouse anyway. This can happen when there is no marital property or debts, no kids, and no need for support; or where there will be no legal opposition because your spouse is long gone, or just doesn't care.

What has to get done. To complete an uncontested case, you have only one or two steps to get your divorce:

> **Draft your agreement.** If your case will be uncontested because you have an agreement, your settlement agreement has to be drafted in a legally sound form that meets legal requirements in your state, then you sign it (chapter 6, step 10, *How to put your agreement in writing*).

> **Complete the paperwork.** In every uncontested divorce, with or without an agreement, you have to go through some paperwork and red tape to get your judgment.

C. Cases with agreements

If you are negotiating your own agreement, you will want to get the details of the agreement worked out and stated very clearly in an informal writing before you make the formal settlement agreement. There are two basic approaches for doing this: the Memo of Understanding, or the more formal Proposed Agreement. The primary difference is style; use one or both, whatever works.

These informal writings are not intended to be a binding contract. You don't want to make a binding contract at this point because you might get it wrong or one of you might have a change of mind. In early stages of divorce negotiations, especially if emotions are still running high, it's not unusual to have a change of mind and it takes a lot of pressure off the negotiations if both parties know it's okay to rethink and renegotiate decisions. It is much better to renegotiate now rather than litigate later over a hasty agreement. When you write down terms in your memo or proposal, be sure to use clear, specific language and be as thorough, detailed and complete as possible.

Memo of Understanding. While negotiating with your spouse, whenever you reach any agreement, even a partial or temporary one,

It is much better to renegotiate now rather than litigate later over a hasty agreement.

make a memo of what you have agreed to as soon as possible, right on the spot if you can. Put a heading, "Memo of Understanding" at the top and start with, "Our current understanding of our agreement is as follows:" then you write down the terms, sign it and each keep a copy. The memo of understanding is a record of the current stage of your negotiation and it eventually becomes the worksheet for drafting a legal and binding settlement agreement.

Proposed Agreement. A different style is for the spouses to send each other written proposed terms to be considered or discussed. The heading is, "Proposed Terms," and you begin with something like, "I propose we settle on the following terms." Keep exchanging proposals and discussing the points until you reach terms that you can both approve.

The terms of your settlement agreement will become the terms of your judgment, so you want to get it done exactly right.

Binding contract. Once your agreement is stable, complete and settled, you next get it drawn up (drafted) in the form of a legally correct settlement agreement. Then you sign it. Then it is binding. If a lot of property is involved, one or both of you may want to see a lawyer—perhaps the same lawyer at the same time—before you sign a binding agreement. This is to make sure you understand every aspect of the agreement and haven't left out some language or term that is required by the laws of your state, or anything important, or used wording that won't be enforceable. Let the lawyer improve the wording and raise other considerations, but don't let anyone talk you out of the agreements you have made without getting at least one other opinion.

How to do it. How does your agreement get turned into a legal document that works? Well, you either do it yourself or you get professional help. Remember, the terms of your settlement agreement (SA) will become the terms of your judgment, so you want to get it done exactly right. This agreement might be the most important transaction of your life, financially and personally, so you want to know it is legally sound. Drafting a settlement agreement is a very technical craft. The language has to be excellent and unambiguous so you don't have two possible interpretations of any term. It has to be complete and legally correct, otherwise it might be weak or defective. If some legal requirement is overlooked, it might not work correctly.

Can you safely draft a settlement agreement entirely by yourself or should you get help? The answer is, "What have you got to lose?"

- If you haven't got much property or income, then you haven't got much to lose by doing everything yourself. You can't afford much help anyway, so you'll have to struggle along the best you can on your own.

- If you have enough income or property to worry about, it might not be a good idea to draft your own agreement. You need to make sure everything is done right and it's probably worth it for you to get some help. Here's one way to think about it: add up the value of all your property and add to that the amount of all your debts then add the value of all future support payments. Compare that figure with the cost of professional help and a contract that is done right.

Can you safely draft a settlement agreement entirely by yourself or should you get help? The answer is, "What have you got to lose?"

The sample agreement on the CD can help you think of terms to discuss and language to use in your informal writing. Resources and services you can use to get your agreement drafted are discussed below in section E.

D. Red tape and paperwork

By the time you sign your agreement, you might already have started your divorce with a petition (or complaint), or maybe not. Either way, you have more red tape to go through.

Can you do the red tape and paperwork yourself? Yes, you absolutely can—if there is a reliable book or kit for your state. See section E below. Hundreds of thousands of people do it themselves every year using books and kits that are specifically for their state. It's not *really* difficult, not exactly, not much worse than doing your own income tax the first time. But it can be tedious and a big nuisance.

Should you get professional help? Ask yourself two questions:

- Can you afford to pay a few hundred dollars?
- What else could you be doing with your time?

If you can afford it, and unless you would enjoy doing it yourself, it would probably be better to get someone else to take care of the red tape and paperwork for you. Give yourself a treat—get this load off your shoulders. You'd be better off spending the time on yourself, visiting your kids, building yourself a new life. On the other hand, maybe you'd rather have a paperwork hobby for awhile.

If you can afford it, and unless you would enjoy doing it yourself, it would probably be better to get someone else to take care of the red tape and paperwork for you.

E. Who can help?

Books. Start by looking for a recent, reliable self-help book on the divorce laws of your state, like my own *How to Do Your Own Divorce in California* and *How to Do Your Own Divorce in Texas*. These books have been published and continually revised since 1971 and 1980 respectively. They work.

Many other states have self-help divorce books but it might not be easy to tell how good they are, so contact the reference librarian at a large library in your state and ask for recommendations, or ask at the courthouse where there is a law library that is open to the public and ask the librarian there if he/she can recommend a reliable book for your state. Another option would be to go to a book store or library and search their Books In Print catalog under "Divorce," where you will find a section of state-by-state listings. Avoid books that claim to be good in all 50 states or many states—it isn't true as every state is different. You don't want an old book that has not kept up with changes, so check the date of printing. If you can find a good book, this might be all you need.

Paralegals and divorce typing services. Another way that lawyer-less divorces get done is with the help of a divorce typing service, sometimes called paralegals or Legal Document Assistants in California. The theory is that you know exactly what you want and merely hire secretarial assistance to prepare and process your paperwork.

No formal training is required to run a divorce typing service, so don't expect reliable legal advice. It is important that *you* be informed and know exactly what you want. It would not be safe to have a divorce typing service draft any but the simplest settlement agreement unless you have a fairly simple, low-value case and your settlement agreement is just like one in a reliable divorce book or kit for your state.

Before you hire someone, find out how long they have been in business, talk to them, ask for references and really check them out.

Most paralegals or divorce typing services keep ads running in the personal classified section of their local newspapers or in the yellow pages under "Divorce Assistance" or some similar heading. Before you hire someone, find out how long they have been in business, talk to them, ask for references and really check them out.

Internet forms sites. There are two types of divorce forms sites and I recommend that you avoid both of them unless someone you know in your state has recently had a good result. If the site is selling forms that you download and fill out, the problem is that you can't tell in advance if the forms are suitable and I've seen too many sites where they are simply useless. Other sites sell an automated form filling service where you put in your information and they supposedly produce forms for you. All the ones I've seen are very difficult to use because you can't tell what you're doing or why you're doing it, what the meaning is of checking some box one way or another. You can't back out and get an overview. The information provided to guide you through filling out the forms is utterly inadequate.

Divorce Helpline. In California, the best help comes from Divorce Helpline, a new kind of law firm that exists only to help people get through divorce without fighting in court. Their attorneys are expert at helping people solve problems and reach settlement. They offer legal information, advice, help with negotiation and mediation, drafting settlement agreements and doing all of your paperwork. Divorce Helpline works by phone throughout California or at offices in San Jose, San Francisco, San Rafael, Oakland, Walnut Creek, Santa Cruz, Sacramento, Roseville, Folsom, Nevada City, Los Angeles, Encino, Irvine and San Diego. They offer fixed fees for services and will work with both spouses if you want them to. If you are in California, call (800) 359-7004.

Be prepared, know what's going on, supervise and manage your own case. That's what works best.

Lawyers. You might, of course, decide to have a lawyer handle your divorce from start to finish. Many people still do. This costs a *lot* more but might be necessary in cases with unavoidable conflict, an abusive spouse, or a very high degree of complexity. Chapter 7 is about choosing and using a lawyer.

Take care that lawyerly techniques do not increase the conflict or complexity of your case, and that you get no more legal action than you really need. Be prepared, know what's going on, supervise and manage your own case. That's what works best. You can also hire an attorney just to draft your settlement agreement. This kind of job should be done at a flat rate. Call around and compare prices.

In some cities, there are cheap lawyers who run divorce mills but, here as anywhere, you frequently get what you pay for. If they do not complicate your case and promote more legal work for themselves, they will essentially be doing the work of a divorce typist for a higher price. Cheap lawyers can't take the time to help you understand your case; they are notorious for not returning your calls. If they get into a conflict with a well-paid attorney, they can't keep up the same level of attention and will be working your case at a disadvantage.

You should only hire an attorney who specializes in family law and, unless your spouse is an abuser or you have an emergency such as one of those discussed in chapter 5B, choose one who is primarily a mediator.

Foreign divorces. If anyone offers to sell you a fast, cheap divorce from the Dominican Republic, or anywhere else outside of your state, and if they say you don't have to live there or even go there, you should be extremely suspicious. Foreign divorces that can be bought without either spouse going there are probably not worth the price of the paper and they definitely can't be used to get valid orders concerning property, child custody or support.

You should only hire an attorney who specializes in family law.

9

HOW TO WIN (AND SURVIVE) A LEGAL BATTLE

IF YOU HAVE TO FIGHT, you might as well learn how to do it effectively, so welcome to the Battle Group. Notice that the title above says "legal" battle—you do not need to battle on a personal or emotional level to win a legal battle. This chapter is where you learn how to control a legal battle when you can't (or don't want to) avoid one, how to battle efficiently and effectively, and how to minimize damage.

You do not need to battle on a personal or emotional level to win a legal battle.

A. How to deal with extreme conflict

Is your spouse an abuser? Highly controlling? Alcoholic? For extreme cases, there are legal remedies (restraining orders), and for all cases there are practical things that you can and *must* do for yourself. This is not about how to reach agreement—these are strategies for self-defense. Mental and physical abuse must be fought and never tolerated. You need specialized assistance from domestic violence counselors and support groups, possibly a shelter. Ask the police agencies nearest you for references.

Restraining orders. The legal remedy for domestic harassment and violence is a restraining order—an order from the court, served personally on your spouse, forbidding certain conduct. Restraining orders are available in any divorce (see chapter 4A, *Keeping the peace*). Where there has been physical harm to you or your children or where future harm is threatened, you can have your spouse ordered to move out and stay away from the family residence. Child visitation can be ordered for specific times and places, away from your home, or, in bad cases, under supervision. It takes very clear proof of danger or detriment to the child to forbid visitation altogether. In extreme cases, where there is clear evidence of imminent danger, some states permit orders to be issued *ex parte*—without notice to or participation of your spouse—which are binding only until a hearing can be held and more orders issued after hearing both sides. You should retain an attorney to get your restraining orders.

Don't hesitate to call the police if you are the victim of serious domestic harassment or violence, and keep calling them.

Here's the good news: over 85% of all restraining orders are adhered to. Being served with orders from a court seems to have a good effect on most abusers. More to the point, they now know that you are serious about not being a victim. Is your spouse the kind of person who will respect a court order? Will he or she care about the police coming out or being dragged into court and talked to sternly by a judge? Does your spouse have a reputation, money or property to protect? Will your spouse, in the heat of rage or hatred, ignore the threat or reality of police presence?

When you request restraining orders as part of your divorce action, you can also take that opportunity to request temporary orders for support, custody, or visitation that will set the terms of your separation until a full-scale trial is held or a settlement is reached. Temporary orders can be very useful if you need them to stabilize your case or get support coming in.

Police. If you have a restraining order, be sure to file it with your local police. This can put them under extra pressure to protect you. But whether you have court orders or not, don't hesitate to call the police if you are the victim of serious domestic harassment or violence, and *keep* calling them. At the very least, you will be building a case and developing evidence.

You should be aware of the practical realities of police intervention. The police might be an unreliable source of help in domestic situations, although this will vary from place to place. They have been accused of prejudice and sexism, but whether or not that is true, their conduct is also based on years of frustrating and dangerous experience. Police are far more likely to get hurt and less likely to do any good in domestic disputes than any other kind of case. This issue has received a great deal of public attention, so police agencies now tend to have standards for dealing with domestic violence. Some departments have officers specially trained in family crisis intervention. Ask responding officers if they can refer you to available spouse abuse shelters, support groups or relevant community services agencies. Call your local police, talk to them about your problem and see what their attitude is and in what way they are willing to help. Start a record in their files.

Self-help and other practical considerations. In extreme cases, where the abuser will not respond to a court order, you will need to hide yourself and your children, possibly get away to another community. In any case of extreme physical abuse or mental control, you should seek help. Spouse abuse is a very common problem so you are not unique or alone. Nearly every community has professionals, agencies, and family support groups that have a lot of special knowledge and experience with domestic conflict. They can almost certainly help you. To find a local support group, ask a pastor, call the police department or a social services agency. If one group isn't what you want, try another. Maybe you can get help from friends and family, possibly have someone move in with you for a while, or get a roommate (a big one). One obvious practical solution is to move away, either for good or at least until things cool down. Or change all the locks, bar the windows and get an unlisted phone number. Or get a big dog. Or take self-defense classes. If necessary, hide—it may be better than being someone's easy target. The main thing is this: do whatever you must to create your own peace and safety; do not depend solely on police or court orders to solve your problem.

Do whatever you must to create your own peace and safety; do not depend solely on police or court orders to solve your problem.

The best kind of help is the help you give yourself. The only thing you can control in life is your own attitude, actions and reactions, so start there. What part do you play in provocation or in being a victim? Understanding these things does not mean you give up and roll over, but it does mean learning to express yourself clearly and not to provoke. In most disturbed relationships, there is some pattern of action and reaction that builds to an eruption. Try to understand your part and learn how to stop the cycle. In no way do I mean that you bear any responsibility for being abused, but that in some cases it is possible to learn not to supply the trigger that starts the abuse or the responses that sustain it.

B. Damage control

If you end up in a battle, it is essential that you understand what you are getting into, then do everything possible to minimize the damage and protect yourself and your children.

You've already read about how expensive a legal battle is and how emotionally destructive it can be, so you know that you don't want to get into a legal battle if you can possibly avoid it. On the other hand, you should never surrender your rights or your self respect in order to avoid a fight. If you end up in a battle, it is essential that you understand what you are getting into, then do everything possible to minimize the damage and protect yourself and your children.

At the beginning of every flight, commercial airlines tell parents that they must always put on their own oxygen mask first, then take care of their children. You can't help a child if you pass out in the process. Same with divorce—you have to be okay before you can help anyone else. So, the first thing you do to protect your kids from harm in a divorce battle is to protect yourself—to develop and maintain your own sense of well-being.

Protecting yourself

The issues in a divorce conflict are almost always emotional ones that get played out in terms of property, money and children. As a tool of emotional warfare, the legal battle is the biggest button a spouse can push, equivalent to launching armies or deadly missiles. You are inviting terrible harm to yourself to whatever extent your legal battle is an extension of the emotional conflict you have been conducting with your mate all along.

The most effective defense is to keep business and emotions separate. Think of the divorce battle as strictly business and run it according to reason and practical considerations. If your spouse gets confused and trapped in an emotional conflict, don't react and don't get involved in it at that level. If your spouse or spouse's attorney uses tactics that are upsetting, don't give them the satisfaction of letting it upset you. Read the suggestions in chapter 6, step 6 for keeping the divorce on a business level.

To survive a legal battle with minimum damage, you must free yourself *unilaterally* from the old patterns that you and your Ex were trapped in. Never mind what he/she does or says—that's not your concern now—your job is to get out of it from your end. That means dismantling a part of your own internal process. Psychological traps like self-blame or blaming your spouse (see chapter 3) are like cement blocks on your legs—they will drag you down for sure. You have to free yourself from the old emotional battle and conduct your legal battle as a piece of business.

To survive a legal battle with minimum damage, you must free yourself unilaterally from the old patterns that you and your Ex were trapped in.

One thing you can do to minimize emotional damage to yourself is like an incantation or a prayer that can protect you. Repeat this over and over to yourself as you prepare for battle:

"I will do what's right, I will do what I must, I will do what I can, and I will do my best, but I will not worry about the rest—it is out of my hands and my well-being does not depend on it."

Do what's right. To get through a battle relatively unscathed, you will need the strength that comes from a clear conscience and moral certainty.

- You must be certain that you want only what is rightfully yours and what is best for the children. Is what you want within the range of probable outcomes—is it *clearly* supported by the facts and the rules of law? Be sure to get more than one lawyer's opinion before you fight.

- You must be very clear that you are not acting out of anger, guilt, fear or greed—that you are not seeking revenge, not trying to punish or control your spouse. You must be certain that you are not merely continuing the old emotional conflict.

You will be protected from emotional damage by the strength that comes from knowing in your heart that what you are doing is right and unavoidable—that you have made every effort to be flexible. Without this, the legal battle can turn your life into pure hell.

You should never feel guilty for insisting on your rights or for refusing to sacrifice your self-respect.

Do what you must. You must know that you have done everything in your power to avoid this battle. It should be perfectly clear that in order to protect your rights, you have exhausted all other alternatives and have no better choice than to go to the lawyers and courts. You should never feel guilty for insisting on your rights or for refusing to sacrifice your self-respect. On the other hand— while you don't want to give in just to have it over with—it is perfectly rational to decide to buy peace of mind by giving up something you would have to fight for. Some things just aren't worth the fight. Either decision is honorable.

Do what you can. We all live within the limitations of what is possible. There is no blame for failing to achieve any goal, only for failing to make the effort and to use whatever talents and resources that are available to you. If you have a right or a child to protect or some dignity to preserve and you fail to make the effort, then you have not done what you can.

Do your best. You can't control others and you can't control most events; you can only do your best. Like everyone else out there, you are an imperfect and fallible human being, so there's no sense in punishing yourself if you occasionally fall short of perfection. If things don't go your way, you don't have to blame yourself if you know that you gave it your best effort. Instead, give yourself a reward and take some credit for your good intentions and for having tried so hard.

Don't worry about the rest. If you do what's right, what you must, what you can, and give it your best, you will discharge all personal obligations in the matter. This is like the ancient practice of writing troubles and prayers on paper that you burn or cast into a river. You have committed your case into the unfathomable processes of the legal system, so the matter is out of your hands and the outcome is no longer in your control. There's no point in worrying about it or being attached to it.

Whenever you get caught up in conflict or feel ground down by it, repeat this a few times: "I have done what's right, I did what I had to, I did what I could, I've done my best, so I will not worry about the rest—it's out of my hands and I don't depend on it."

It is very important to adopt an attitude and a life-style that does not depend on the outcome of the battle or on anything your spouse says or does. This doesn't mean you shouldn't care about it or try your best, but don't let your well-being depend on the outcome. While the legal battle drags on—and it may be quite a long time—you should explore other avenues and build a foundation with the other resources in your life. The legal wheel is turning and the chips may or may not come to you when it stops. Meanwhile, get on with building your life.

If you do what's right, what you must, what you can, and give it your best, you will discharge all personal obligations in the matter.

C. Protecting your children

Go back and read the last pages of chapter 3, *Rules of the Road #2—Getting your children through a tough time.*

Studies show that harm to children is more closely related to conflict after the divorce. Everyone has conflict before and during a divorce, and children can recover from short-term upset. But if you want to protect your children, get finished with the conflict and resolve it, at least within yourself, as quickly as possible, so at least one parent will be okay. This will teach your child that problems can be resolved, that things can be well again after a storm.

To protect the essential parent-child relationship, you have to insulate children from your own conflict with their other parent.

Children need their relationship with both parents. There is a bonding that cannot easily be replaced by a surrogate parent or stepparent. To protect the essential parent-child relationship, you have to insulate children from your own conflict with their other parent. The divorce is not their problem; it's yours. Being a bad wife or husband does not make your spouse a bad parent. So, don't hold the children hostage—they are not pawns or bartering pieces in your game. In the area of custody and visitation, don't bargain with your spouse on any other basis than what will give your children the most stability and the best contact with both parents.

The worst thing for the child of a broken home is feeling responsible for the breakup and feeling that loving one parent is a betrayal of the other. These feelings cause children intense stress and insecurity. To protect your child from almost unbearable pain, don't say anything bad about the other parent in front of the child; don't undermine or interfere in any way with the child's relationship with or love for the other parent; don't put the child in a position of having to take sides. Do encourage every possible kind of constructive relationship your child can have with your ex-mate. Let the children know that you are happy when they have a good, loving time with their other parent.

Kids can really get on your nerves at a time like this and single parenting is enough to overwhelm any normal person. You are not Superman or She-Ra, the Princess of Power, and kids are not designed to be raised by one lone person. You need help and support, and you need time off from the kids. Make a point of getting help from family, friends and the many parent support groups and family service agencies throughout the United States. Get references to groups in your area through temples, churches or social service agencies.

D. Winning strategies—hardball or soft?

What does "winning" mean to you? Think about it. You have certain goals to pursue and rights to protect—that's all. The first and most important thing you do to "win" is to immediately stop thinking about winning and your spouse losing. Divorce isn't that kind of contest and a relationship is not a battlefield. If you think that way, you are setting yourself up to be a loser. Separate yourself from the contest emotionally and conduct this battle strictly as a piece of business.

The first and most important thing you do to "win" is to immediately stop thinking about winning and your spouse losing.

Never start a divorce contest on the strength of a single opinion. Take your case around for a variety of advice. This is essential: don't skimp at this critical step in your case. Ask a lawyer if your demands are reasonable under the law. Ask yourself if your goals are worth the price of the battle.

What *are* your goals for this contest? Whatever your other goals, there is one that should always have top priority—to *negotiate* an acceptable settlement. Everything you and your attorney do should be aimed at getting your spouse and your spouse's attorney into good-faith negotiations that will lead to an agreement that you can both accept. Okay, what strategy do you use to do that?

There are two basic types of divorce strategy, defensive and aggressive. Which should you use? When anxious hikers asked the old woodsman what to do if they ran into a bear, he explained that one school of thought holds that you must stand perfectly still until the bear goes away, but other experts say you're better off banging pots, screaming and waving your arms. Studies show that both schools are right about half the time . . . it all depends on the bear. In divorce, everything depends on you and your spouse until the lawyers come in, then it depends on four personalities. It gets hard to work out or second-guess what is best—something that only gets clear after it's all over, after the bear has done its thing and gone away.

Hardball or softball? Softball is a civilized, easygoing approach to the legal contest. Your purpose is only to stick to what you think is right and, if necessary, let some judge decide. It is a decision to disagree peacefully, to let the lawyers do their job and the legal process take its course. If you can't agree, why get upset? Let the judge decide. Hardball, on the other hand, is a tough, aggressive strategy. If your spouse is being bad or is likely to cheat, you have to defend your rights very forcefully—and you might have to show some teeth. If your spouse is the one who starts being legally aggressive, you have a choice—respond in kind or be defensive.

If your spouse is the one who starts being legally aggressive, you have a choice— respond in kind or be defensive.

Aggressive cases are those where you are on the offensive. You move fast; you hire an aggressive lawyer to strike hard. You fire off a full range of legal motions and go to hearings to freeze accounts, put your spouse under court orders to behave, and set rigid visitation schedules for children. You send out volumes of legal interrogatories (questions) and you demand or subpoena boxes of documents and paperwork. Aggression costs a great deal of money and can destroy future hopes for good personal and co-parenting relationships. It can damage your children, maybe permanently. But, in extreme cases—as when dealing with an abuser or compulsive controller—it might be necessary.

One goal might be to get what you have been denied: honest information, your fair share of the community property, access to your children, relief from abuse, and the like. Another goal may be to make a dramatic statement to your mate—a cold splash of legal realism as shock therapy. You are showing teeth in the hopes that it will lead to negotiation. However, aggression is risky business that can backfire. It depends on the temperament of your spouse *and* your spouse's attorney. Avoid the trap of using legal aggression to punish or harass your spouse—that sword cuts two ways and you *will* get hurt. It isn't worth it. You should use aggression only if forced into it by circumstances beyond your control.

To conduct an aggressive case, you will be looking for an aggressive lawyer who is also experienced, bright, tough, and tenacious. Spend some time interviewing various lawyers about their philosophies and attitudes. If, for example, a lawyer is eager to attack, that lawyer may be just as quick to attack you if a difference of opinion arises. Look for someone who goes to battle reluctantly, who is always looking for a way to cool the battle down, but who can punch it out if necessary. Read more about choosing your lawyer in chapter 7.

You should use aggression only if forced into it by circumstances beyond your control.

Defensive cases are those where your spouse is on the attack, coming on hard and strong. Your choice here is either to conduct a stubborn defense or to go on the offensive. If you do the least possible to protect your position, you conserve your energy and money while waiting for your mate's team to run out of steam. A quiet defense can make it easier to negotiate an agreement later. A good defense is almost always more comfortable and less expensive. Let them do the work; let them bark and growl; you can just rely on the facts and the legal process.

If your mate's attorney is unusually aggressive or they play dirty tricks, like making the case unnecessarily expensive with a flood of paperwork and motions in court, you might decide to play their game. If you counterattack and drag your mate personally through some depositions and hearings, maybe you'll convince your mate to negotiate. But first, ask some questions of yourself and of your attorney:

- Have they got the facts right?
- Does the law support their position?
- Are they aiming anywhere near the probable outcome?
- Is your mate's position or personality vulnerable?
- Is this going to be worth the expense?
- What's the advantage of striking back compared to just letting it go to court? What do you have to gain? What can you lose?

Even if you get into an aggressive battle, you should always be looking for ways to cool it down and to negotiate an agreement.

The strategy you choose always depends on knowing very clearly what your goals are. Then you consider the facts and circumstances, and the personalities of the people—you, your spouse, your attorneys. Then you make your decisions and choices.

Obviously, softball is the better game. It costs less and hurts less. If you don't have to worry about bad or dishonest behavior, let the lawyers negotiate and the judge decide what can't be agreed. Even if you get into an aggressive battle, you should always be looking for ways to cool it down and to negotiate an agreement.

E. How to fight effectively at less expense

1. **Plan and prepare.** The person who is better prepared and organized will generally do better in negotiation, mediation or court. Read chapter 5E and chapter 6, step 6.

   When you go to see a lawyer, you don't want to waste any time—it costs too much. You should know your goals, be familiar with all the facts of your case, and know as specifically as possible what you want to talk about with the attorney. Send the attorney a letter before you go in, detailing exactly what you want to discuss, and include copies of relevant documents. That gives the lawyer time to absorb your information and gives you a chance to see if the lawyer bothers to prepare for the conference. Organize your papers and thoughts. Make an agenda before you go. Keep notes on every discussion and keep track of time spent on the phone or in the office so you can compare it to the itemized billing.

2. **Know exactly what you want from the battle.** The most important part of preparation for battle is thought. Don't go to war without it. Think about your facts, your life, and get very detailed and specific about what you want: property, support, future relationships for yourself and your children, life goals and values. Sometimes all you want at first is more information that your spouse won't give you, or verification of what has been given. Your lawyer can get information under oath. At some point, you will have all the information there is, then you will have to decide what you ultimately want.

   The most important part of preparation for battle is thought. Don't go to war without it.

   Planning your battle strategy—even to the type of attorney you choose—depends on a clear understanding of what you want to accomplish in the battle. What property do you want? How much support? How much do you care about future relations between you and your spouse or the emotional well-being of your children and their relationship with their other parent? Read chapters 5E and 6, step 6.

3. **Try to narrow the issues.** Before you get into a battle and during the battle, do whatever you can to narrow the issues. This means trying to agree with your spouse, in writing, on as many issues as possible, then agree that you disagree on the remaining issues and those you will let the court decide. A battle is much more efficient when conducted on a narrow front. Be very cautious about taking advice to broaden the battle. It can indeed strengthen your bargaining position if you ask for much more than you want or attack an issue you

don't care about, but it can also stimulate the opposition, undermine your credibility, and prolong the battle.

4. **Set the tone of the battle.** If you care at all about keeping the level of conflict as low as possible, then be sure to keep your spouse informed at all times and well ahead of time about what you and your lawyer are doing and why you are doing it. This helps to minimize unpleasant surprises, misunderstandings and overreaction, especially if your spouse returns the favor. It helps to keep the background lines of communications open. Communicate by letter to avoid arguments; keep copies. Remember, most cases eventually get settled by the spouses between themselves, not by their lawyers, so you will be better off for trying to keep communication lines open.

Most cases eventually get settled by the spouses between themselves, not by their lawyers, so you will be better off for trying to keep communication lines open.

5. **Carefully choose the right lawyer.** It might be okay to rely on the first attorney you interview for advice, but that's not good enough for a battle. It is very important to take your case around to several lawyers to get a variety of opinions and attitudes before you choose the one you want. Don't economize at the wrong time; paying for these extra interviews can save you a fortune later. Read chapter 7, think about your objectives, then decide what lawyer you are going to work with.

6. **Make it clear that you are in charge of your case.** This is your life and you have to live with any consequences of the divorce action, so it is reasonable—and important—that you be ultimately in charge of your own case. You want to hire the lawyer's knowledge and experience; you very much want to listen to the lawyer's good advice; but you expect to be part of any decisions that affect the tone and strategy of the case. You will be ultimately responsible.

Tell the lawyer that you would like copies of all papers and correspondence, and that you expect to be kept informed of every step in the action. Also make it clear that you expect your phone calls to be returned as soon as possible, no later than the next working day. In return, you have to reassure the lawyer that you will not be one of those clients that makes frivolous calls.

7. **Don't hesitate to switch attorneys.** If your attorney's services turn out to be unsatisfactory, you should send a letter with specific details of what the problem is and what changes you want made. If there is no improvement, start looking for another attorney. See chapter 7F, *How to fire your attorney*. It's surprisingly easy.

This is your life and you have to live with any consequences of the divorce action, so it is reasonable—and important—that you be ultimately in charge of your own case.

APPENDIX

– How to get the information you need

THERE ARE PRACTICAL THINGS you can do that will help your case, build your sense of confidence, save money and reduce the feeling that you need an attorney or court action. On the personal level, chapter 3 is about things you can do to reduce upset, anger and fears, while chapter 6 is entirely devoted to steps you can take to move away from litigation and toward negotiation or mediation.

Getting the facts

This might be the most important, useful, confidence-building, money-saving thing you can do. Gathering and organizing your personal and financial information must be done sooner or later and sooner is much better. If you were ever to seek legal advice or assistance, your attorney will need the facts, so why pay the attorney hundreds or thousands to guide you through fact-gathering when you can do it yourself for free using the worksheets on the CD in the back of this book?

Ideally, spouses will exchange information openly and fully. This helps build trust and confidence, and in most states it's the law, so you might as well just go ahead and do it. If information is not exchanged freely and you can't get it through any of the self-help methods described below, you will probably end up in court with attorneys doing very expensive discovery work. Give your spouse a copy of this book and discuss this section.

Here's a partial list of important information and documents you want:

- Federal and state tax returns for the last three years
- Bank records for three years: passbooks, statements, and checkbooks
- Credit card statements for the past three years
- Records of loans, debts, obligations of any kind
- Real estate deeds and mortgage papers, lease or rental agreements
- Insurance papers, policies, statements
- Auto license numbers, registration, and insurance information
- Driver's license numbers for both you and your spouse
- Statements and records for stock accounts, mutual funds, pension plans
- Books and records for a private practice or any self-employment activity
- Books and records for any rentals
- Birth certificates for you, your spouse, and the children
- Social Security numbers for you, your spouse, and the children
- Health insurance cards, copies of medical records
- Your passport and any immigration documents
- Family address books, calendars

Pay special attention to financial records in the year before your spouse got the idea there might be a divorce to see if any unusual transfers were made.

Do you already have these things? If you have facts and documents and your spouse doesn't, here's a fine opportunity to build trust. Don't give away your last copy, but otherwise make sure your spouse has free access to all records and information in your possession. No tricks, because they usually backfire and can cost you a lot.

Hard-to-find assets. Deferred compensation (income your spouse received and put in a savings-type plan on which income tax is not paid) will not appear on tax returns, or in a bank account, and might not appear on pay stubs—for example, if the contributions are not being made currently. These records must be obtained from your spouse or from your spouse's employer through a subpoena.

Tax-free income—for example, income from municipal bonds—will probably not appear on a tax return. To locate such an asset, you probably have to get a copy of the checks used to buy the asset, a statement, or find other written evidence.

Easy ways to get information

When you collect information, make two or three copies of everything. If you borrowed (with or without permission) your spouse's records to copy, return originals that you don't personally need. One set goes to your lawyer (if you ever get one), one set is for your working files, and one should be put in a very safe place: a safe-deposit box, storage locker, or some other secure place your spouse can't get into. Do not hide things in a house the two of you share or in the trunk of your car.

Ask your spouse. Of course, the simplest thing is to obtain copies of documents from your spouse—just ask nicely. But if you don't want your spouse to know you are collecting documents, or if your spouse is not cooperative, or if you think your spouse can't be trusted, you can obtain a surprising amount of information acting completely on your own.

Collect what you have access to right now. You have a right to all information about your marital estate and you actually own any records related to joint accounts or documents that have your name on them. If you have access to the house or office make photocopies of every document you can find.

The home computer. If your spouse uses a computer and you have access to it, make sure you get a copy of all important or useful data on it. If you don't know how to do this safely, find a computer consultant to do it for you. Make duplicate copies of data and put one copy somewhere safe away from your home or office. If your spouse has a password on the computer and you're not worried about starting a war, take the entire computer box and put it where your spouse can't get it. Later you can file a motion asking the court to order your spouse to give you the password, or ask the court to order a disinterested third party to hold the computer, receive the password from your spouse, and copy all information from it before the computer goes back into your spouse's control. Taking a computer is a hostile act which you must weigh against the possibility of losing whatever information might be on that computer that could be hidden from you later if things don't go well.

Tax returns. You have a legal right to a copy of any joint income tax return that was signed by both you and your spouse. It is best to have complete, certified copies of your returns and all amended returns, together with all schedules and attachments, not just the form 1040. You can get certified copies of federal returns from the Internal Revenue Service and state returns from your state's tax agency.

You can get copies from the IRS of any forms you signed. Use IRS form 4506 and send it with a check for the amount indicated on the form. The IRS sometimes provides copies within a month, but sometimes they send you a letter that basically says, "We can't find your tax return; ask again in 60 days if you really want a copy." Therefore, you need to make your written request to the IRS long before you actually must have the copy in your possession as you may have to make more than one request.

If you want a copy of your state income tax return, contact your state's tax agency. As with the IRS, you must send a check to pay for the copies and for certification.

Accountant. If you used a professional to prepare tax returns, you can ask for copies from recent years, but most do not keep W-2 forms and they cannot certify copies. Even if your tax preparer is a great friend of your spouse, he/she is obligated by law to give you a copy of any joint return with your name on it. When you first get your hands on copies, look at the first page of each return and see if it refers to any schedules or attachments. If it does, make sure you have the attachments. For example, if it shows a figure next to "Schedule E," make sure you actually have Schedule E. Ask whoever gave you the return for Schedule E and point out that the return shows that one exists. This is usually sufficient to get someone to cough up the schedule. You want all pages and every schedule of each return.

Locate property on the Internet. The Internet is a great way to locate people, personal property (such as cars, boats, airplanes), and real estate. Such searches are becoming easier and more useful. You can ask an attorney or private investigator who has Lexis-Nexis service to do a search for you, or check law libraries near you to see if they have it, or you can pay for an account and search on your own. With Lexis, an attorney can look up your spouse's name and see (among other things) if any property titles are associated with it.

Look up deeds at the County Recorder's Office. Every county has an office, often called the Recorder's Office, where they keep property records. Ask any real estate agent or at the county clerk's office. Go to this office and look up your name and your spouse's names in an index. The index gives you the information you need to obtain a copy of the deed at the Recorder's office.

Get bank statements. For joint accounts, you can get copies of statements from banks and other financial institutions by asking and paying a fee. Banks keep copies of all deposit slips, deposits, and photocopies of the front and back of all checks for about six years. The bank will not give you copies of statements for accounts that are only in the name of your spouse. Unless your spouse will give them to you voluntarily, you will have to go to court to discover the information.

Look for hidden assets. Once you have copies of tax returns and deeds, read them carefully, even if you have a lawyer. For example, Schedule B of the tax return lists interest income which might help you discover hidden bank accounts. A deed will show the company or attorney who recorded the deed, and you can contact them to obtain copies of the closing statement issued when the property was purchased. If you have significant property or complicated finances, these documents might not be sufficient. But without at least this much, you do not have enough information to make intelligent decisions in your divorce.

Personally review all records even if you have a lawyer. If your lawyer gets copies of your spouse's bank records or other statements, you should personally review everything as you might notice things the lawyer cannot. For example, an accountant working for the wife's divorce lawyer reviewed the husband's business records and concluded that everything was in order. But when the wife reviewed the records, she saw that the husband's payroll listed his girlfriend who did not work in the company. The accountant was good, but only the spouse could tell the difference.

INDEX